About the author

Laura Flecha was born in Rockville, Maryland. She spent some years living in Sedona, Arizona, and Memphis, Tennessee, and now resides in Poolesville, Maryland. She attained her Masters in Writing from Zanvyl Krieger School of Arts and Sciences at Johns Hopkins University.

Laura works as a publications and production manager for the American Gastroenterological

Association's medical journals, *Gastroenterology* and *Techniques and Innovations in Gastrointestinal Endoscopy*.

Laura's main passion in writing is poetry with a focus on women's issues and subjects that can be difficult to talk about. As she was brought up Tibetan Buddhist, her writing sometimes reflects Eastern concepts, though it always blends with Western thought and experiences. Her hope is that her writing brings comfort to those who may face similar challenges, and perhaps provide insight or a shared understanding of human nature.

Laura adores spending time on her farmette with her husband, two daughters, son, goldendoodle, chickens, and ducks.

READY ROOM

LAURA FLECHA

READY ROOM

Vanguard Press

A CIP catalogue record for this title is
available from the British Library.

ISBN 978 1 80016 230 3

*Vanguard Press is an imprint of
Pegasus Elliot MacKenzie Publishers Ltd.*
www.pegasuspublishers.com

First Published in 2022

**Vanguard Press
Sheraton House Castle Park
Cambridge England**

Printed & Bound in Great Britain

Dedication

To Vic Goldie, my first creative writing professor, who pulled my writing voice out from within me. To Ed Perlman, my most recent professor, who helped refine my writing voice. To my family, who has supported my writing endeavors and encouraged me to keep going, in writing and in life.

Contents

Tsuru

The planes are paper cranes, and they appear
To glide from children's hands, like origami
Slicing out shapes from introspective skies
Whose vastness stretches over wishes flying.

I watch the paper cranes and wish there was
A place where I could fly, to feel the glinting
Silver that pierces clouds in knife-like ways.
Sometimes I just want things to hurt, to know

That I'm alive and not too close to numb.
I read a book about a dying girl,
Thousands of paper cranes, a trip to heaven.
I wonder about these paper cranes today.

I hear Sadako's prayers for "peace on earth",
Folded with colored kami, thousands of
Creases invoking birds of vibrant dye.
If they could take me, I would go, surrender.

The Thinning of Rainbows

I meet you at the musty gas station.
Rain brings out the smell of hard-working men.
I call you Grease Monkey, my temptation
Fueled by force and fumes, shaken now and then.
I used to play a game where I would try
To color code people like cheap mood rings.
I hop in your diesel, not shy, all spry.
Down gravel roads, your intimacy stings.
I let you trespass me; you say "for keeps."
I watch myself, oblivious to pain,
Partake in love like oil that spills and seeps
Into dismantled hearts, 'neath skies of rain.
I swallow hard, thinking how I'd paint you,
Pretending not to feel the way I do.

Early Still

Rainfall. Late night.
Sound of moist air
Moving through a window fan
That's barely doing its job.
But I forgive it.
Night's too hot even for it to work.
Just come in from the barn,
Shoveling horse manure from stalls.
There is no other place I could see myself.
No other place than on the front porch,
The sound of rain hitting the tin,
Tapping the pond and saying goodnight,
While I smoke a cigarette and miss you.
Time seems to be distant,
Just like this small town to me.
Just as though my life were moving away
Just as the storm's coming in.
The air is thick, the thunder rolls.
I resist to give in to a night like this,
Though it pulls me into a childhood
Dream with no umbrella.
My father is long asleep, and my stepmom
Becomes my best, maybe only friend.
I wait for daybreak, for the dew level to drop.
I wait for my fan to start working
So I can fall asleep.

Behind the Ribcage

Inside every girl
Lies a corner where she cries
For all that seeps in.

Come Dawn

Early morning.
Whippoorwills are up,
And dawn has not yet come.
I patiently wait for her arrival.
The pond is still and the grass
Is layered with dew.
Reason to put off mowing for a few hours.
I help my dad load his truck,
And part of me wants to go build
A house with him today.
Stop on the way for coffee and more smokes,
Then meet the other workers on the job site.
But I know I've got to stay.
My pigs are still sleeping.
When dawn wakes them
They'll squeal for pellets,
And I'll feed them and muck the pen.
Spray the cement, put down straw.
And maybe if it needs it,
Fill up their mud wallow
With well water from the hose.
I say goodbye to my dad.
He climbs in the truck and pulls away
Down the gravel drive.
Air's too thick with moisture for dust
The fog has pulled a veil over the pasture

Sissy will be out soon
To feed the horses who stand
Like still ghosts in the field.
Maybe I'll help her; I could use a friend.

One Gift I'd Give

Her voice is sharp, dense
In sound, no subtlety, yet
Mistaken for shy.

She turns up damp rocks
And underneath her fear is
Confidence the way

Water wears on and
Doesn't consider its path;
It just moves along.

Cliffs reside some day
In her future where water
Releases downward.

She waits for this like
Someone standing under a
Muted waterfall,

One who knows the rush
Will come, waits with arms, face up,
A smile river wide.

Grown from the Cabbage Patch

I.

His mama never knew what dress to wear
To church, "Run out and roll the windows up.
The rain is starting up again, ya hear?"
His sister always fell on pavement, scraped
Her chin or knees, the accidents unbandaged.

His name was Shane. He tucked in his collared shirt
For Sunday school. His mama made his sister
Go to choir, though she had no voice.
"God damn, don't got no dresses,"
His mama would say.
His papa wasn't dressed for church on Sundays.

Shane's sister always looked so sad. I used
To call her Emma, the name she took when we
Played dolls. We spent our days in make believe,
Dressing our dolls in cut-up dishrags and scraps.
Pretending made the grownup world feel softer.

I was always such a doll, so I was told.
A compliment, I guess. "A Cabbage Patch Kid,"
His mama used to call me, "Bloomed from the field."
Truth is, the soil around here
Has been starved for years;
There's nothing in that field. Dead roots and dust.

II.

Their yellow house had a back-room closet, tucked
Away from heavy boots on wooden floorboards.
We'd hide behind the hanging clothes, read Keats,
A Snowy Day, and dream of getting lost
In mounds of white, in innocence and wonder.

The first time — Emma was in church and five
Years old — they say it's too young but it's not,
Because I was there, and she was praying out loud,
Repeating words on rosary, her blonde
Hair plastered to her cheeks with tears. She prayed

But no one heard, not even God. Not then.
It'd be a few more years and lots more scrapes
And bruises, lots more hiding before they found
Her hanging in the back room, behind the clothes,
A spot like an annex, cloaked, enclosed, and safe.

I didn't see Shane after that, nor step
Another foot inside the yellow house.
It haunts me still how Emma never would
See beyond the dusty fields that yielded nothing.
Often, I pray she's found her snowy day.

Generational Curves

I bent over to have my back examined for the curve,
My spine a thin strip of ribbon.
I could see the gym teacher's shoes,
Her legs like logs, robust and stable.
I imagined she would be good at shot put or softball.
I was good at high jump, long jump, track.
I chose to run through, not only in P.E.
But in all aspects of my life.
It was what I knew and understood.
Like the other girls, my body was thin.
Being in high school, I, of course, had hit puberty,
But I had no curves and few features.
There was no evidence except for the fragility
Of my paper doll body.
If I had lived by the sea,
I might be blown by the coastal winds,
Across the blue tide that changed
With the day of the month.
I had been in arms of boys,
Friends who saw me as their dew,
And when their sunlight hit, I glistened,
Flashing smiles that had been passed down to me
From all the women who came before.
We disempowered ourselves by eating
Very little and speaking wistfully.
We laid around the house in various rooms,
Switching chairs and moods,

The sitting room, the living room,
The den, the upstairs library.
We talked to boys on the phone, giggling,
Fracturing our demeanor,
Hiding the muteness, shoulders slightly convex
Like the bulb of a tulip.
We worried about how we said things,
If we said too much,
When to speak and when to catch our words
Before breaking silenced air.
We cared because we were women,
And that's what women before us had done.
So without contemplation, we did the same.
Our mothers were dolls once but now
Had grown and had curves,
And their mouths were now more
For words than for kissing.
They no longer needed protection, and the boys
Who caught their generational smiles
Had now grown into men, sometimes of infidelity
Or a silenced unfulfillment.
We had hopes, of course, that our boys
Would never become this,
That we could please them more, that something
In history and in us had changed,
That their palms would only stroke *our* curves
And taste only *our* smiles.
Fourteen, we puffed on cigarettes,
Pulling in the smoke.

Eating very little, very little now.
Our hope then was, of course, that we would not fear
the curves as we grew.
But we did so, and so grew the starvation,
The deprivation,
The severance of our fragile bones.
The gym teacher felt my back and said nothing.
She placed her hand on my collar bone when she had
finished feeling the ribbon,
Straightened my back to standing,
"Stand taller," she said,
"You have nothing to mute to.
You have nothing to hide."
I flashed a smile to her east, perhaps understanding
From one curve of the earth to another,
That being a silenced woman was not a woman at all,
But a girl who was too afraid to shine.
And with a love of life lit small
And my sense of self growing out,
Filling in the concaved space
Between me and other women,
I looked up and cast my shattered syllables
In a bone-setting yet contoured voice.
"Okay," is all I said, but we both heard so much more.

Happy Continuation Day

I was born with a disease.
Curable? No.
Treatable? So they tell me.
I have yet to be changed
By the medicine they give.

I was born in an ocean, current
Stronger than me.
I was born in a teardrop.
Binding me together are
Molecules vibrating,
Bouncing off each other.

I was born with no skin,
With my mind rushing.
I was born without the ability
To slow things down,
Without the ability for so many things.
I was born with eyes that see,
But with a disabled heart.

I was born sunburnt and fire-parched,
Wind-torn, earth-cracked, and water flooded.
Born in the knot of the heartwood of a tree
Surrounded by layer upon layer.
Holding me apart from the world,
This wall is as force-filled as steel.

I was born in a snowflake,
Different from all the rest.
If only I could melt
And become like everyone else.

I was born in hurt.
I was born sad.
I was never born.
I am only continuing.

The Funnies

I envy
Garfield, the way
He stretches out in long
Pulls, with every stretch, thinking
Of all the nothings he has to do that day.

I haven't always envied Garfield, maybe
Just today, and yesterday,
And maybe all the days
I've been a
Grownup.

Surely
I didn't envy
Garfield when I was a child,
Slurping milk from a cereal bowl
Like a kitten, giggling over what project Odie

Was conjuring up, a Saturday on the farm
Stretched before me. Those days where the
Outside air would breathe me
In, lead me to
The creek,

Where the
Rocks were slick,
But falling only meant

Cooling my skin, the silt squishing
Between my toes, finding a rock, which

Was the coolest rock I'd ever seen. Laughing
Because I had to trace my steps
Back home along the dirt
Path, wet and muddy,
Enter

The house
Leaving water tracks
With little feet, making
My parents laugh as I clumsily
Made my tracks through childhood. It's funny how

I don't read the funnies anymore — and I laugh less —
And I would never connect the two.

Just a Boy

He's just a boy who's grown a bit,
Not how you'd remember him.
He's starting to come to
From all the mess life has put him through.
Wondering what it's all worth,
He watches with his long stares.
Don't mistake him for knowing
Less than he does.
This boy would surprise you.
He's more than any boy I know.
His mind is a labyrinth,
But he's not trying to trick you.

He's pure, doesn't engage in games.
His smile reaches across time.
His tears teach me forgiveness
And help him to move on.
He's cleansing his body
Of what's been kept inside for years.
He's sweating now, looking like
A young boy climbing
A ladder out of a pool.
Beads of salty water drip from his mind.

He's letting go of the people
Who gave him life: Mother, Father.
He's forgiving what he can't change.

He's accepting the boy in him who is sad,
Accepting that the days have moved on
Too quickly for him to keep up.
I'm sitting on the counter, feet dangling, arms open.
He's peeling an inner skin;
It falls to the floor beneath his feet.
That still ache from yesterday.
He's singing now, a song I haven't heard in years.
It feels like a whisper from a long-ago friend.
It is in this song that he's finally able
To communicate what has never been said.

Samatha

I want to run through the desert.
Not like the time I was running from you,
Barefoot, crushing flora, dodging tumbleweed,
Cracking the baked layer of the soft, red sand.
Not like the day I jumped out of the car
Because it seemed a safer chance to take.
I want to run through the desert
Where no one is around,
Where the only sound is a bird's wings flapping,
Swishing, pushing air, moving with the Earth's turn.

This time, I wouldn't be trying to escape, but rather
To find myself in a place of stillness;
The only feeling– my chest pumping air as though
I am running just as fast as the world is spinning.
I am running because when I run,
My mind slips into calm abiding.
I run until my body falls away.
Some nights my dreams of running
Keep my mind awake.
I'm running through the elements,
Through wind and rain.
I'm focusing on a point; this point is all around me.

Thoughts stream away like beads of sweat,
And a natural awareness emerges.
It's not about appearance or expectations anymore,

Or how much one can give or get.
Not about perception or clinging to "you" or "I".
I'm not running from these things,
Nor towards something new.
They simply fall away, because their nature is empty,
And without basis, they are non-existent.
Running is like meditation,
Watching the breath, training the mind,
And letting go of what is unnecessary.

This Deserves Form

They wine and dine, discuss red pears and port.
I smile, fair and subtle, keep confined
With rosy cheeks, starry-eyed dreams of import.

"No baby 'til you're thirty-five," aborts
The dreams I may have had on some cloud nine.
They whine, my eyes dine on red pears and port.

The canvas hangs in distance, an art of sorts.
"The red pear" this, "The red pear" that, defined
With rosy skin, delectable taste of import.

His father squeezes my arm and then reports
That I'm a bone (again); I can't opine.
They wine and dine, discuss red pears and port.

The red pear hangs, discolored and deformed,
Curved, robust and blushing, yet refined
With rose pastels, fruitful dreams of import.

They aren't aware that I'm with child, the court
Cut short by this abruptly forming spine.
They wine and dine, dismiss red pears and port
With rosy cheeks; we all have dreams of import.

Roseate

My father hasn't called yet.
The leaves prepare for winter.
Two months will soon be three,
And the colored leaves will turn
To mold, crushed into the ground.
My face blushes, and my nose turns to rose.
I try and warm myself by a fire,
But teardrops put the fire out.
I become too tired to hold
My weary eyes open.
My breath is frozen,
White smoke pouring forth.
The ruins from my lost memories
Drift through the snow roads.
My father is gone.
I grow colder and colder,
Frostbite consumes me.
A shiver is all that's left.
I whisper a tune he used to hum.
I whisper it into my skin,
Wishing for warmth
And a comfort only a father can give.

Response to Hills

I will dress my baby in white
White if it's a girl
White if it's a boy
Give it life covered and draped
In sheen, white satin
Soft against its skin
This is after all the screaming
It has heard through my skin
All the yelling about being impregnated
All the concerned calls from my father
Asking if I'm eating right
If I quit smoking
If you're sticking around
If we're getting along
If it will last
After all the breaks slammed on
While you're driving
After the shoving and bruises
Have healed
I will dress my baby in white
White if it's a girl
White if it's a boy

Changing Stages

"I am changing."
He said, "You are a change,"
As he touched my body gently.

I flash back to the surgery room.
My face is in a white pillow.
White walls, white sheets, white lights,
And tan men with face masks.

"Do you feel your vitality?" He asks me
After pricking my abdomen.
"Yeah," I answer flatly.

The Principles and Practices of Natural Childbirth

My baby has been ripped from me.
Do I feel my vitality?

The first cry is heard through Stadol and numbness.
I don't see my baby.
I'm taken to a room. Separation sets in.

Light contractions still occurring as he adjusts my legs.
The network chiropractor.
The nurses rub my stomach with force.

"This will bring the heat back in, stop the bleeding."

Hours of trying to nurse. Failure. Too weak to mother.

I'm numb from the waist down.
Tummy cold, chest heavy, shoulders slumped.
Do I feel my vitality?

I am a change.

Childbirth Without Fear

They tie my wrists down.
I'm whisked away to the operating room.

Painless Childbirth

I'm crying. The catheter disappears.

I'm shaking uncontrollably
In a room with two women.
I ask if it's normal,
And warm blankets are placed over me.
And my body is never the same.

I am the change.

Room empty of flowers.
I will never do anything this hard again.

Twenty-three hours of Pitocin.
I am contracting, but it's not working.

Failure.

I walk the hallway, long and sterile.
People smile as I pull my IV.

He calls the baby "girl". That's what he called me
When he was falling in love too.

I'm injected with Stadol. The drug settles in.
I fall into a trip, an allergic reaction.
My focal point becomes my only sight.
She is strong in my changing room,
My changing mind.

"This will calm her down." I don't hear them.
I'm wheeled away and down.
Into the elevator, up with a gust. My eyes are heavy.
I've been riding waves of the ocean.
Every four hours, trustily
The Percocet and Motrin are administered.

"You tell me when you've reached your goal."
Physical, emotional trauma: I circle 10.
Difficult birth. Depression. Loss of appetite.
"I Love Lucy" and "7th Heaven".

Discursive thoughts. I am grieving.
I took a class; I learned my breathing.
I am no longer pregnant, but I still touch my stomach.
It's cold, cold. Not used to being empty.

Red Line

The New Jersey train rumbles, smooth in few spots.
I stare at my newborn baby in the seat across from me.
She is adjusting well, much better than me.
I am trying to change; she is changing without trying.
I look at her, look out the window,
At her, out the window. And back.

The city is dirt. Soot-covered and in disarray.
I love it.

Just think, this morning
I was hiding in a corner from you.

In New York I remember best
Sitting in the park with you.
Vendors passing muttered, "Smoke, coke, fake ID."
We pass another train. I can see the city in the
distance.
The train is slowing,
Must have been twenty-eight minutes.
Philadelphia.

When I was a child,
I used to sing out the window of the car,
Taking no account if anyone was listening.

The woman who just exited the train walks gracefully.

She makes me want to starve myself.
I want to walk like her.
The conductor puffs smoke before we leave again.

If I could clear my head for one minute,
I'd know what I was doing.

Delaware.
Baltimore. Finally familiar territory.
Metro Red Line. All the way to Shady Grove.

Good champagne is Korbel. We'll get some tonight.

Why are people afraid to stare into each other's eyes?
Children still believe they can be invisible.
I am a child.

Through tunnel, arrive at Shady Grove, end of line.
We unload our baby gear, enter terminal, disoriented,
Like stepping off a moving walkway.
The sun hits our faces as we emerge from the station.

I'm thinking of my father,
Who I can't remember very well.
I'm thinking of him lifting me up on his shoulders
To touch the sky,
The feel of the sun on our faces.
Same day, different life. Approaching
Yet never reaching.

Ink Blotching

"You should ah – take a road trip
For a few days, relax."
And so we drove through the desert,
And in a roadside town
I picked the 'flu up from some grimy restaurant
With a sign out front advertising family dining.
Why, when you open the door to a family restaurant,
Are you hit with stale cigarette smoke?
I guess family dining to a restaurant
Means crayons with paper placemats to drawn on.
My seven-month-old baby wouldn't be amused
With such things yet.
So I gave her a spoon and let her bang on the table,
And she was satisfied.

Our waitress had bleached-blonde hair,
And I imagined she imagined
Being whisked away by some boy,
Anything to leave this dried-out land.
She probably gave us the 'flu
As we drove through that town,
Serving it up alongside Salisbury steak and salt gravy.
If I were her, I'd marry any young man
Who promised me escape.

At the end of our road trip was my bed.
The 'flu was in me

Like bleeding black ink from a busted pen.
My clothes hung on me,
And I sweat out blotches of ink.
When the days became mounds of my lying torpid,
I went to see a doctor.
I lay on the floor in the waiting room.
I felt my inmost channels shift, and I began to fall.
Is this death?

At last, the doctor called me back,
And I walked to his office like a dead bone.
He was a classic doc: white hair dusted to the side,
Medium build, calming voice.
I let him take my temp and listen to my breathing.
"Well – you got the 'flu. Nothing we can do for you."
Is that it? And if I die? Can I sue?
I was carried home and slept the afternoon away,
And the next day, and the next.

Maybe it was my fever dropping,
But I was coming back to.
I drew a bath to soak and imagined
The ink running through my skin,
Draining into the sewer and turning
Into some sort of heat,
Because no energy is ever lost.
I saw the heat thaw the body of someone,

Shivering against a bleak brick wall,
Allowing him for a moment to feel warmth.
And my illness was gone.

Romney, WV

Reminds me of West Virginia,
But how many times can you write
About places you've been

West Virginia at a bowling alley with grandparents.
Bowling shoes –
And I can't remember much more.

Just the grime and cigarette smoke
And the smile on my dad's face.
The look read 'tricky'
As I attempted to knock down pins.

Bowling was one of our things,
Like ice-skating,
Something we did together
For as far as I can remember back.
I'm sure he wanted it that way.

If I'm lucky, I'll be able
To create that with my children.

And it will be bowling alleys in
West Virginia all over again.
My face will read 'tricky' as my girls

Roll the ball towards the pins
With hardly any effort.

They'll remember shoes,
Bowling shoes, just like me.

Oceanic Eyes

My cheeks were puffy and rouge from crying,
And the barber looked at me and knew
And didn't say much.
I dropped into the swivel chair like Pickup Sticks
Released from hands.
The barber scratched and tugged at my tresses
As my tears were pushed undersea.
I was merely a shell being scrubbed by salty water,
Used to the pain but everchanging under pressure.
As he sleeked and trimmed my hair,
At first you could see my chin
From beneath the seaweed,
Then my flushed cheeks, and lastly my eyes,
Those which unearthed me,
And I could retain no secrets.

Through These Eyes

As I turned my shoulder to walk away,
I heard him whisper,
"We're so lucky," as he slipped his wife into his arms,
Crying still and choking on brimming salty tears,
Thinking of his father who he lost suddenly and
His child that came into his life just as suddenly.
But I'm thinking I'm lucky too
Because my daughter has shown me that
The world needs compassion. She has opened doors
In my eyes that allow me to see what I couldn't before.
Through our suffering we have gained a gift that
We can share by gently opening doors
In others' eyes too.
It might make them cry,
Might cause them to lie awake in sleepless nights.
It might sadden and disenchant
Their view of this world.
But it just might plant in them a seed
That can grow to change the world,
Through the eyes of compassion.

One Droplet

We're running with bouquets of soft scent,
With petals that pivot and rotate like a salsa dress,
Blossoms peeling off stems onto pavement.
With fireworks making sounds of bombs behind us,
Buddy runs faster, cries louder, and an older girl says
It must be the tubes in his ears.
She said she knew a girl who had cancer in her school.
She says her hair fell out for a month,
And kids laughed at her,
But when it grew back, she was the most beautiful.
She says my daughter, Asia, is so beautiful
With a soft head,
While the moon above us illuminates her.
I deal with chemo by imagining
It is the purest of medicines, a holy nectar.
Tonight, a torchlight on the river's top water
Searches for an adrift ardor.
I imagine a droplet of water
Evolving into a thousand droplets,
Containing the nutrients to cure
A thousand sentient beings.
May I be just one droplet and give myself
Wholly to another.

Dox

I'm in the hospital in the mesh chair. It's Sunday in the
medicine room, and the staff is skeletal like my
daughter's cheeks when she's pale and not smiling and
has been on the dripping IV for a week. The room
smells sterile, like loss of appetite. They keep sending
me Ensures in the mail because I've gotten so thin, but
I haven't noticed and don't see what they see. After the
nurse leaves, my routine begins. I get up and touch the
bag of red doxorubicin. It looks good enough to drink,
but there's a warning on the bag not to touch without
gloves. If it goes inside my daughter, I can surely
touch it from the outside. I run my fingers down the
bag and pray that it does magic. I envision it going into
her and healing every part, making every cell perfect
and useful. I say the Medicine Buddha prayer, which I
will chant for hours until I hear it instead of my fears.
Dox is the color of the red balloon, the color of the
riverboat, the color of the trim around the hospital, the
color of blood, the color of blushing cheeks, the color
of power, of convertibles massaged by breeze, the
color of my daughter's lips, the color of the first
comforter my husband and I bought together, the color
of the red rocks from where she was born, the color of
hearts, the color of healing, hope, weekly roundtables
with varying chemo drugs, of Shirley Temples when
you're a child and it's the fanciest drink ever, the best
flavor of Skittles and blow pops and the ripest cherries

on the tree, the color of transfusions, of skinned knees and infections, of slapped cheek syndrome and the isolation entrance to the hospital, of red envelopes and boxes in the mail, of teddy bears and great big bows, the tongue of my first golden retriever puppy, the color of mixed emotions and tempers and tears. It's the color I'd give away in trade for something not so loud. It's the color I'll remember most from the medicine room.

Losing What Were Precious Jewels

I lost my wedding ring on a sweltry day in Memphis,
On a day I searched through parched grass
On the banks of the Mississippi,
It was an off day from chemo, and we went to hear
Music in the streets of downtown.
My daughter said she missed her Montessori school
As she watched the other kids with her longing eyes.
She didn't understand why she couldn't go.
And her understanding of her loss of hair
Was the simple one we had given her.

I lost my wedding ring in between the pool
And tanning oil on my hands,
And sitting on a swing in front
Of Miss Cordelia's Market,
Sipping not-quite-cold beer from brown tinted bottles.
The kids balanced across the curb,
Imagining a tightrope they'd seen
At the circus the night before
When a clown took the time
To peek up at my daughter from behind a wall,
His cheery colored bulb nose
Touching her delicate face,
A face that had lost its smile until that moment.

I lost my wedding ring in Memphis heat,
Under a blues band drawing a crowd.

Our strained family, us, standing in a battlefield,
The only weapons the tools in our minds.
I lost it between hidden tensions
Of a husband and wife,
With all the odds against us; we tried.
Tried to stand in the wind, in the storm,
In the heat, in the war.

Luray I

The cabin rests on forty acres of open space,
The fertile land giving birth to a peach orchard.
My body is like this entire valley of mountainous land,
And the womb, an open space.
The fever arrives when the sun
Turns in the autumn sky.
Hidden springs pour out of jagged rocks,
Creating a wetland beneath the fallen leaves.
The auburn and burnt golden colored leaves,
Like the forceful tides of my femininity,
Turn, tumultuous, doing as they want,
Leaving my body under quilts,
Under the forest's canopy.
At least the view is nice as the sun casts rays,
Creating shadows in my wood-knotted room.
I wait for this to pass, breaking open fertile earth,
Clearing an open space in the center of my body,
A place of sacred ground, a cavern
Buried deep in the earth's rocks and plates.
Later we run on deer tracks
In the clay and gravel roads
Along the river letting go beside us,
Atop maple leaves that are subtly
Changing from moist to dry.
I leave the orchard, not forgiving myself here.
I keep running down the gravel bend
Trying not to picture the undeveloped skin,

Trying not to think that I was once undeveloped flesh.
I leave it there and with it I leave
A sense of claiming my body back.
The swelling will go down now,
The cramping will subside,
The spring will empty its waters.
And because I don't want this to mean nothing to me,
I call the miscarry Luray.

ER

We sat in the ER,
Rain
  Drizzling
    Down
The wide windows,
Our hands together
Laughing and cracking

Unfitting jokes.

Autumn Squill

There was a walk along the pier in fall
The week we stayed beside the lake, adrift.
St. Michael's rental, walls and sheets of white,
My face still bruised a tender, purple squill.
I watched the boats go where I wanted to—

Away. Away from a love not tender-full
Into some soothing waters, calm abiding.
But I had grown too used to pain with love,
And so I stayed, entrusting me with him.
But know what I remember most of all?

The sound of bumping boats as we climbed
In canoes as bright as embers glow. We set
Beneath the sun, toward town, away from all
Our worries haunting us and causing sweats
That woke us, kept us in the night as dark

As blind can be. Remember? As we soared
In murky sea blue-green, we lost ourselves
So slyly that we didn't even squint.

Dreaming in Gingerbread

The first frost of this year blankets the roofs,
Creating the look of a neighborhood
Of gingerbread houses.
And as the sun envelops the valley,
The scent of powdered sugar frosting
Suffuses the air, in through the cracked window
Of our sugar bread home.
I outline my eyes in midnight,
But the gray disks still
Glimmer through the blackness.
I'm lying on the wood floor,
Hands propping my head up.
He's putting his head to my chest,
Listening to the ocean and silver fish splashing.
He's tasting gumdrops on my breasts,
Wishing he could capture
The fire burning juniper in my heart.
He breathes it in and envisions
A snow-layered path winding through the woods,
Him and I kissing and shivering
And touching warmth between skins,
The only thing holding our emotions
From drizzling into each other,
Like honey into steaming tea.
Pomegranate tea that shudders my tongue

And forces my body to sigh.
All thoughts unify and dissipate and recreate only love,
Descending like snowflakes from a moonlit sky,
Defrosting on our figures waltzing in dim light.

The Thaw

Winter was filled with slushy streets and
Drunken nights at the hookah bar,
Nights that tasted of apricot and sounded
Of the jingle of belly dancers' hips.
No one thought that there was a lack of happiness.
It was perhaps when things started to thaw,
The scents of comfort started to fade.
Winter tasted like roasted roots
And home-baked cookies.
We were trying new recipes
And trying to get life to work out.
I was sprinkling with sugar and pressing
Peanut butter dough with crisscrosses.
Scrubbing mud off wood floors
And polishing until the salt was washed out.
We were sledding with rosy cheeks down hills,
Holding little hands inside the sleeves of snow suits.
We were watching snow melt
Into the ponds and streams,
While underneath, where frozen ground lay,
There was the changing and dying
And shedding and new life budding,
Something that would break open, release,
And force us to grow.

Dirty Laundry

I'm not in his life.
I'm falling all around it like
The clothes around my hamper.
He's tripping on the clothes
And cussing and saying
He doesn't like my ways.
He says he'll find another date
For Valentine's Day, and I tell him
"Go ahead," thinking that
There's nothing left to save anyway.
He thinks I've met someone new,
But I think he wants to meet someone new.
Neither of us is sated,
Have never reached satiety,
Nor do we know how.
So I keep throwing my emotions around,
Hoping one of these times he'll get it.
But he just keeps mishandling and
Stumbling on me and me on him.
He washes my delicates on
A rigorous cycle; he puts holes
Where they don't belong.
I don't rock him hard enough,
Don't give him what he wants.
I cry to him when there's no one home,
And wonder why the door is locked,
I check the windows to crawl inside,

Scraping my knees and bruising my sides.
I'm screaming, he's thrashing.
The thunder is here, and the rain is approaching.
Yet the only shelter we can see is beneath
Each other's pride, uncertainty, and mistakes.

Cyclone

He's shaving in the mirror and nicks
The skin on his jaw,
And he's thinking of us and all
The things we could have done differently.
I'm watching him through the doorway
As I pour the coffee,
But he doesn't know I'm staring at him,
And that I'm thinking the same thing.
He's grabbing for his toothbrush,
Then brushing his teeth with stress,
Spitting out pink blood.
He spits the way he used to when he was angry,
As if the person he was angry with
Was standing face to face with him.
I can taste the animosity in my own mouth
As I'm mixing in the cream and burning my tongue.
He sees me in the background and
I try to turn my eyes off him,
But not quickly enough,
Because he knows now that I have seen him
In this moment where he thinks
All I see in him is weakness.
But he has never understood how
I think crying is a strength.
As a tear falls from his cheek,
He's reaching for the mirror
And pulling it off the wall,

Taking it above his head and then
Throwing it down so that no reflection can be seen.
Is it me he wishes he was shattering?
Is it me he wants to make disappear?
As he turns around, I know
I should get out of the way.
But I just stand there,
Thinking force will bring him some temporary relief,
Thinking I can hold my own.
My face is turned head on into the storm,
My empty expression braces and reinforces
For the waves that I know are imminent.
Love's painful and confusing and pushes me
As if I'm being whipped in a cyclone's funnel.
If only I could reach the center,
And maybe find stillness.
I'm falling to the ground,
Losing my footing, losing sight, consciousness.
But unlike the mirror, I am still in one piece, yet —
The mirror can only be shattered once.

Inner War

I'm on the ground, breathing
You in out of the carpet,
Back curved like fetus.
I build myself up with pushups,
Thinking of beating you up
Or at least throwing some good punches.
And I cry louder and harder, stripping
My contacts from my eyes
Like a layer of smooth snakeskin,
And I can't see. But does it matter?
Could I see before?
I am lost in a puddle on the floor
With nothing making sense,
And the room is spinning
Like a bad carnival ride.
I'm screaming to get off because I'm getting
Sick of the gut feeling of it all collapsing
And everything falling away,
Left with only this mess of a mind of mine.
Because when it comes down to it
Our own minds are all we have
I am a casualty from my inner war,
Bleeding and slaughtered
On unthinkable turf.

Confession

That's it.
I've said it before
Like a mantra
Like getting sick of winter
And wanting spring
Sick of spring
Then wanting summer
I've said it
That I take my heart back
That I end the drive
The expectations
The one-way longing
I end this now
Yeah, I've said it
And I've meant it
And I've contemplated
And thought out
But yes, let him off
And no, never left
And so you call me
Whatever it is that
You call me to let me know
That I should have left
That I'm scared and
Just like a book
Reacting just like every woman
And I wish I could say

I am not every woman
But in fact I am
The very expression
The very curvature
The very tender impact
The very saliva and labor
The very fluidity
And solidarity
Of every mind
Of every woman

Wayward

Cold winters
Lie in front of me.
There's a turning in my face
From a fair peach to a blushing rose.
My calm hands begin to shake.
My voice goes from soft to silent,
And a tamed lion can be seen
Shaded in my eyes.
This organ called my heart
Is melted caramel over heat
An apple is dipped and immersed,
And I await your devouring:
Teeth crushing, juice spilling,
A scent of spring or new beginnings.
The loneliness of waiting,
The fear of spoiling,
Putting my happiness in someone
Who is, in fact, wayward.
But I am finding
That I am much the same.

Stamina

In the fall, before the marriage turned,
I'd swim in crisp air with our potential on my mind.
I offered myself completely to the thought
Of accomplishment with perseverance.
Just stepping off the battlefield,
It was fresh like the air.
We were left changed, but unmarked.
My feet hit the ground as if jumping down
From high above and landing perfectly
Or walking away from a should-have-been
Fatal car crash, unscathed.

But fall froze to winter with words like
"This is not my dream.
I'm not accomplishing anything."
And I tried to mop it up, failing miserably,
Now thinking of Mickey in *Fantasia*.
I was swept under a rug, so heavy
On me, I couldn't move.
Paralyzed by the weight, my voice
Became a whisper in winter's cold.
The longer I didn't take action, the more I disappeared.
Pent up like a child in a playpen,
Not old enough to talk,
But old enough to run away.

I don't know where the strength came from.

What is stamina?
It's almost—
An unconscious inner push
When you've nearly given up, a squirm,
Then a movement,
And then you rein that movement
And mount the strength, so you can ride away.

Over Beer and Dollar Sushi

The trees are the color of Kristen,
Silver tossing, bracing limbs,
Ground saturated.
Glints of birds appear to be flying out of the sun,
Clouds like footprints, also walking away.

We walk through sticky rice
To a table with high booths.
I tell him I'm not good with chopsticks,
Forgetting that a short time ago,
He knew all my mannerisms,
All my glances, pouts, smiles in my eyes.
And I his.

It's disenchanting the way marriage begins
And ends with the signing of a paper,
Portraying the life of a flower.
Through youthful florescence
To the wilting rain of petals,
Dropping in un-concentrated loss,
A reflection of impermanence.

I've been skinned of familiar;
I am raw and uncontained.
These days don't exist outside distractions.
I wonder if he feels the same
As we both look down to the sashimi on our plates,

To the paperwork we are here
To initial with our shared last name,
To the goodbye we are supposed to say.

Baby Blue Tears

His thumbs are pressed into his eyes now,
Palms holding his head up,
As the final papers are signed.
I think of gently touching his back
And rubbing my hand over
His pale green button up shirt.
But considering — I don't.
Instead, I start crying, and
I'm wiping the tears from my eyes
Like windshield wipers against glass
In a heavy downpour.
I didn't want it to end this way, and I know he feels
The same when he starts to cry as well.
His tears are falling into his lap,
His lap that cradled both our children as babies.
My earth still shakes when he cries,
And I know this feeling
Within me that wants to end his suffering
Will never cease.
There's a stack of child support cases
On the mediator's desk.
If tears could be stacked, they'd look like this:
Paper holes punched in light blue folders,
Names in illegible signatures,
Agreements to pay for children who never thought
Their parents would live in separate homes.
And then there are the empty dotted lines

Of someone missing someone.
If only the tears in this world could always
Motivate our compassionate activity.
We are nine stories up on Monroe Street,
And though I know this building hasn't fallen,
I have already hit the ground below,
The way an amusement park ride takes you up and
Drops you unexpectedly.

Divorce

You'll hate divorce,
The bumper stickers of the lines of stick figure
Families on mini vans and SUVs.
You'll hate the HOV lane, the Kiss-n-Ride,
The passenger seat in your car,
The other side of your bed.
You'll keep the blinds closed
In your house for a year or two,
Because the sunlight only reminds
You of waking another day
When all you want is the end of each.
You'll see mini vans, remind yourself
Of the divorce rate in the US
And tell yourself it's only a matter of time
Before they downsize to an apartment.
You'll be familiar with 51 Monroe Street
For the child support enforcement office
And the court next door.
You'll understand the importance
Of presenting your case
And know how to talk to lawyers
To make them favor your side.
You'll take handfuls of pills that are supposed
To make you want to
Put a bumper sticker on your car
That says, 'Life is Good'.
But they only make you tired

And numb and want to sleep
Stretched out on your bed
That is too big for only you.
You'll hate your first few dates,
Maybe even the first dozen,
Because all of them
Will either remind you of him
Or be different from him,
And you'll hate them all.
You'll drink old coffee by accident because
You have not had time to do the dishes in a few days,
And there are coffee mugs in every room
And you can't remember where
You placed the fresh one.
You'll hate all the magazines,
Parenting mag, *Family* mag, *Family Circle*,
Because what's the point? You may have been trying
To raise the perfect kid,
But once you're divorced?
You're just trying to keep the kids alive.
You'll hate Saturday morning, Sunday morning,
Monday morning, Friday night.
In fact, you'll just hate them all.
You'll keep your wedding ring around
To make you feel bad, but only after you thought
About pawning it several dozen times for the cash,
But they were all petty offers.
When your wedding song comes on the radio,
Ironically called *Love Suicide*,

You'll listen, maybe sit in silence, then react,
Cry, scream along, and then
Finally change the station.
You'll hate the fact that you still love his family,
And that they still call, they still write,
Still send money on holidays and for accomplishments.
You'll hate the stack of home videos in your bedroom,
But you still watch them.
You'll understand why 'shuffling kids'
Is a good general term to describe the weekends.
You'll forget to water the plants around the house,
Because that was always his job.
They'll hate you before they die,
And then you'll feel bad
And buy more, only for a repeat experience.
You'll be bitter on love,
Then won't believe in love,
Then be terrified of love,
And then fall in love,
But this time more slowly,
Only (perhaps) for a repeat experience.

Home for Rent

I place an ad: Two bedrooms and one bath
With room to stash your heartache far from seen.
The shades can cover all of your mistakes,
With closet space for stacking cardboard dreams
And packages of jaded memories.
The ceiling fans will blow nostalgia out
The windows—waiting for some fresh-start air.
A deadbolt lock to keep him from returning
And crawling back into your life, unsought.
There's wall-to-wall white carpet covering
Foundations built when you were young, in love.
A fully loaded kitchen cooking up
Desserts with sugar, spice, and all things nice.
The in-ground pool shimmers with salty tears.
The sheets will be your tent of solitude,
The blankets tucking loneliness away.
So cuddle up and make this house your home.
Call first to view: 18 Honeycomb.

Haunted

I woke up with thin skin.
Got lost in the ocean again.
Coffee tastes like mud pie,
Pulling me out of my weakest place for assault.
The sheets are like egg yolk
Running broken down my legs.
I keep saying if only easy was a noun
And I could give it to him, then maybe.

I had dreamt of him in a foreign language.
He came up behind me, put his arms around my waist,
And everything made sense.
It was written out like a love letter.
There were pauses to show love and
The point of connection was clear.
Then I realized that I'd forgotten how to use longhand,
And that it had all been written in tears.

When I finally saw the ghost of us,
She was a bloody mess and
Made the sound of bombs dropping.
She keeps living it over and over,
Each time forgetting it's already done.
Each time thinking she can fix this,
And believing so deeply
That she forgets the truth.

Preterit

He said, "I loved you."
And all I heard was the '—ed'
And the coldness of my wedding dress
In a dampened cardboard box
In a landfill somewhere.
I thought about my wedding ring still on the alter,
And the words to wait a year
And reevaluate
And if it would have been different
Had the words been followed,
The tears he wiped when
Our daughter nodded her head
Yes to that wish
Were the same tears I've cried.
They come from the same well,
The same swollen walls
Of a cold heart underground,
Of dreams that weren't 'stored right'.
So eventually you have to discard.
I've heard all the opinions,
But my own is like the bottom of a dress,
Swaying in wind, not so tangible.

September 26th, 2009

The sky cries all day for me, so I don't have to.
I begin to add nutmeg to my coffee
Because winter is coming soon.
We make pancakes for dinner
Because it seems like the right thing to do.
I went to the store for chocolate chips
And then folded them into the batter
So there'd be chocolate in the air.
"Today's the day your dad and I married," I say,
In a matter-of-fact tone, like telling them
It's any other holiday worth celebrating.
"Is today hard for you too?"
I think about calling and whispering to him.
"Or do you not think about the dates anymore?"
The light bulbs burn out in my room all at once
As if telling me I am in the dark.
Aren't we all always in the dark?
I mean, we never really know what one another feel.
Early on, the three of us used to cry at night,
Where's Dad? I don't know.
I want Dad. I want him too.
We spend the day in a downtown DC distraction
With poets and painters,
Storytellers, dreamers, and peacekeepers.
I forgot about the date, about sadness,
And only remembered the all-encompassing
Beauty of words and thoughts.

I held my children's hands all day,
Their tiny palms reaching to mine.
More and more they do things on their own,
And someday they won't need me
For anything but listening and words and hugs.

Hideaway

We'd go there after arguments,
After reconciliation,
At the start of honeymoon stage.
We'd sit under white oaks towering above Oak Creek.
We'd sit in dry air in falling canyon,
Order beers and antipasto salad, dressing on side.
It was to make it better, make new.
We'd give rise to change, create new vows,
And promise to not break.
There was something precious
And worth holding on to.
And anyway, time makes you forget.
And sadness fades, dries like tears.
No questions asked, only answers exchanged
In expressions on our faces.
It was our hideaway.
Though part of me wants to go back,
I no longer need this place.

The Other Half of My Bed

It used to be kisses like blueberries,
Each one varying in flavor and texture.
Used to be summer nights with windows open,
Letting warm scented breeze rush over the two of us.
I couldn't roll over into an empty space, because
His body was always there.
My bed now is divided in two, consisting of
The sliver I leave on the edge for myself,
Sheets that tango with cool blankets of fluff,
And what I call 'the other half'.
On any given day, the other half is filled with junk.
As I lay here tonight, it's my coat and a sweater,
Other articles of clothing heaped in a mound.
Books that I've read just a few sentences out of,
Not enough to get entranced.
Spools of colored thread and needles with small eyes
For patching up emotional breakages and tears.
Tears that have dried into salt flats
Creating visions of water
Like a bleeding desert under Arizona sun.
I hear music from the other half
That sounds like every wedding song
And white doves flying, but if you listen closely,
The music is crying and
Breaking at the seams, every note
More tragic than the last.
Smeared lipstick that plays dress up on my sheets

Telling me the world is pretty and tender
And that longing from the outside won't get me in
Through the window I am peering.
The other side of my bed is empty, day in,
Day out, month in, month out.
And so I fill it with things that matter,
Things with weight,
Books holding wisdom, that if I sleep
Next to them it calms me,
And maybe I'm not so alone.
And if I fill that other half, there's no space for me
To roll over and know that it's just me here,
Night in, night out.
All that's missing is the rhythmic breathing
Of the one I could relate most to.

Letting Go of a Memory

He kisses the top of my head,
And it's random thoughts that come to mind.
This time it's the lot in Michael's Ranch,
Us watching the Arizona sun setting
Beyond the desert hills
The night we sat on the plot of land
Nestled with cactuses and tumbleweed,
Imagining the life we built taking
Form upon the red dirt.
It's these sorts of things that are hardest to let go of,
Not of the house we could have built,
But the memory of that night, licking ice cream,
Skygazing and daydreaming, our hand intertwined.
Planting our daydreams like seeds
So that the roots could dig deep
And a sapling could emerge
With room to rise into a boundless tree.

Wait, wait, wait—
I'm not done there yet.
For if these tears are worth my broken heart healed,
Then I'll trade all these memories for tears.
The most romantic place:
A canyon just north of Sedona.
If you're flying over in a plane, it's the only imprint
On the earth for as far as you can see.
It's where low desert meets high desert,

And they dance with water.
He took me into this canyon, each carrying backpacks
And *tabula rasa* strapped to our hips.

The water runs down sheer red rocks,
And the bark on the trees
Has the scent of ambrosia and brown sugar.
The ferns are taller than us, and we lay
In them to conceal what is ours to share.
We look up to towering oaks whose arms
Create a marquee from the sun.
We keep hiking until we are forced
To wade through this translucent creek,
And the canyon has enveloped us so completely
That we can't hear any outside noise.
The world has truly been left behind,
And for all we know, vanished.
He holds my waist through the water,
His hands on my stomach,
My favorite place for them to be.
While he holds me here, he sings,
Just loud enough for me
To hear his vocals through his whisper,
The song about forever.
His voice trails off at the end of every line,
Maybe a premonition that our forever will fade.

This place we were, the beauty is more
Profound than the Grand Canyon,

It's something Lewis and Clark
Would have stumbled upon and made records of,
Saying something to the nature of what
They had said about the plains:
"I had been led to believe,
That it was barren, sterile and sandy;
But, on the contrary, I found it fertile in the extreme."
Because we unveiled an oasis in the desert,
One that embodies all continents.
And now the pain I feel is as vast as all the continents.
The loneliness, as if the world
Around me has imploded.
The only signs that the canyon
I speak of was an actuality
Are the hieroglyphs etched on my body
And the runes in my mind,
Where once there was a love,
Where once we discovered each other.
And now the song he sung to me I hear,
Whose meaning I now understand,
Forever is not here in the end.

Luray II

My dreams are of my old life most of the time.
Flying erratically, the blackest of crows.
I plant a scarecrow in my mind to keep
My dreams away, but then I cannot sleep
At all. And so I've come away to woods,
A new cabin nestled in the rainy hills.
On saturated ground I run along
The road, outrunning my dreams from nights before.
Under dappled trees. Luray has come to be
A place where I abandon all things heavy.
This time I try to abandon all my dreams,
But haunting me is my empty room back home,
The sound each night, a lonesome cackling crow.
The hours, always long and torturing,
And each crow, circling, carries more regret
Until I'm buried and halfway to my death.
And if I fall asleep, I will be raped
By my dreams, unable to control the stream
Of disarray, then waking up to realize
My blankets caught the tears again. And I'm
Tangled and drenched and swearing that I'll go
Through tragic measures not to fall again.

Shedding the Unnecessary

Taking him out of my life is like
Taking wallpaper off an age-old plaster.
It comes off in pieces.
Like a child picking at a scab on their knee,
I am anxious for him to be gone.

Just Let Me—

I wake up early, the sun hasn't even risen yet.
I push my face into my pillow,
Wishing the day to begin
So the nightmares in my sleep will stop.
I press my palms into my eyes,
Smearing my face like modeling clay.
I think of stretching my legs
And walking to the kitchen,
Rinsing out the glass pot,
Shaking the chocolate grinds into the filter,
Pouring soymilk into a mug and
Waiting for the coffee to brew.
Instead I roll on my side and begin to cry,
The dampened pillow beneath me so familiar.
I'm fighting the thoughts in my head:
If I get up and start the day,
I'll want only to be asleep again.
And if I fall back asleep,
I'll want only for the dreams to end.
So I slip into a state of detachment,
Somewhere between the two.
Neither awake nor asleep,
Neither satisfied nor dissatisfied,
Content nor saddened.

Puddles Dry

She told my mother, before I was born, that sometimes my mom would have to just take me and hold me together. But my mother didn't understand what she meant by this. I am the black spot left in the sky after the star falls. I'm lying in the street after they cut my clothes off. I'm exposed and raw and the street beneath me is flowing, so I become a river and bleed into it and am washed away. My eyes hurt when I open them, like when you open your eyes under water, and everything is stinging and blurry, but you just can't close them because you are seeing into another world. I am the sound of the rustle of the covers on the bed, when all you're trying to do is get comfortable, but you can't stop shifting. It's so subtle, like a whisper that you're not sure you heard. When something's so quiet, it can fade, it can fall apart. And there's nothing left to miss.

Suicide

I have stopped writing.
I have stopped eating.
My stomach has walked away from me,
Leaving an empty space in the center of my body,
Where all my stress and self-hate are.
Tomorrow I will get up and act like I am okay,
Like nothing is wrong, like he's not gone.
And that makes it okay.
But I am not, and I know it.
And isn't that all that matters.
I think about dying.
I think about driving my car fast
And crashing into something.
I think in those last moments
I could feel something.
I could feel the pain that I am housing,
Feel the pain that I am cutting off.
I think I'd be human in those last moments.
I would bleed. I'd be open.
I would cry and ask for help.
Maybe I wouldn't want to die then.
Maybe then, I would change my mind.
And it would be too late.

In My Midnight Room

Some days I don't know who I am. I cope
The best I can. I say, "This too shall pass."
I cling to the thought of fading and hope
It's not another day I'm made of glass,
A glass that fractures, sensitive to light.
I try to undo dreams, un-believe. I fret
Night terrors that have overtaken sight
Of my reality. I dream that regret
Is all I know. It wraps me in a blanket,
Makes me think that loss is comforting, the way
One feels relief when letting go, the threat
No longer near because *everything* is at bay.
"Delusional," I tell the triage doc,
Hoping behind me the forever door will lock.

O Gretel

He boiled the eggs like every morning, not long
enough to toughen the yolk, but that it would still leave
an indentation on the toast as it caught steam rising
from the bread. It was 4:42 and counting as he placed
the sliced cheese and salted ham on the wooden table
with cloth overtop the carved names one couldn't quite
call graffiti but more like callouts. His own was even
there, 'O! Gretel, Kai loves you!' The night they had
chiseled away the wood was the same they had rescued
bottles of Hefeweisen from behind the Schnookeloch
bar and escaped to a room upstairs that had not been
rented. The restaurant was full that evening as the
fireplace told stories in flames and warmed the cheeks
of everyone sipping gluhwein. The crowds had poured
in from the streets after the Christkindlmark had
dwindled down. They had spent the night there,
captives of their emotions, only seventeen but
knowing. The next morning, Gretel lay on the white
sheets with a blanket half covering her. Kai had pulled
it up to her collarbone, then walked to the window that
overlooked the orange rooftops snuggling Heidelberg.
He got dressed in not much, only one layer, but put his
coat on to cross several streets to the Church of the
Holy Spirit. The door to the church looked like it
might be frosted shut, but he pulled against the chill
and threw himself inside the warmth. Inside, he
confessed in the booth that he loved this girl more than

religion. The wooden box was swelled with worries from years of repent, and his own fear found a notch to be kept in.

From behind the screen, the priest simply said, "Son, pray to understand, religion is only a path to guide us with love. Let your love for her teach you how to love all beings."

Kai thought about this now as he often did. He finished setting out the breakfast for the hotel guests. He pressed coffee with hints of hazelnut and, once brewed, climbed the spiral stairs. He opened the door to room 201, sat the mug down, and gave Tapioca, their Bjelkier pup, a pat on the head. She rested beside Gretel and looked up at Kai, sleepy still, but wearing her protector face. He walked to the window, the same one he stood at that morning when he was seventeen, and cracked it. Kai knew Gretel liked to wake up with the contrast of the chill from outside air against her skin and the warmth of the blankets holding in heat. He let her sleep for a minute longer with his hand on her stomach. There was joy for him in letting her sleep as he prepared the day to wake.

He always woke her the same, "O Gretel, love! Leave your dreams with the fading moon and come see the world with me."

This day she joked and smiled as her eyes lay barely visible, "But my dreams encompass all the suns, so let me be." She rolled toward him and kissed his hands. Gretel taught comparative religion at the university. She didn't settle down in any religion *so as to not gather dust*, she would kid. Her method was to take what she found to be wholesome morsels of various religions and make her own loaf. He imagined it would taste similar to Schwarzwaelder Kirschtorte, a cherry-chocolate cake. Often Gret would say, "Before I die, I want to have accomplished some peace outside myself." They often watched sunrises together. After several times of seeing her close her eyes during them, he asked why she did that. She replied, "I offer the beauty of the sunrise to peace. You can see it fill the sky. Then the rays become more than light."

Gretel normally took the late train in the morning, but she had off this day. So Kai had Gitta covering reception, and the two had planned to hike to the Schloss and then wander the Christkindlmark, perhaps ice skate at the rink that had been set up for the festival. They ice skated frequently in winter, for the exhilaration and the heat. They both loved stripping down to only one layer in below freezing temperatures, steam coming from their breath, as if the air was frost and their bodies dawn. They would crash into and whip each other around on the ice as if there were no friction, and only the gravitational force between them. Kai walked downstairs to wait for Gretel to be ready. Tapioca followed, having heard the word 'hike'. Kai met several guests in the dining area as they ate their breakfast. Tapioca gathered attention with her smile and white coat. Kai told a little girl sitting with her parents that Tapioca was a reindeer herder and just visiting for the festival, and that she would be returning to help Santa in the North Pole in a few days. She smiled coyly, and he winked at her.

Gretel came down the spiral staircase, stepping on the narrowest side of each step. She'd come down the stairs the same way since she was a teenager. Her eyes looked at Kai's as if she was sharing a secret he had always been searching for. Kai smiled and breathed out; realizing then that his breath had gone. They wrapped up in scarves and left the Schnookeloch, bracing against each other in the cold. Their eyes teared, and she gave him a pout face as if she was crying. "O Gretel, what's wrong? You can't possibly be sad on a bright, beautiful day like this!" Kai said, sarcastic and serious. The snow fell like glistening sugar, and the sky was powder gray. Kai was right; winter was its own beautiful form. The Schloss was stretching and yawning below the clouds on the mountainside, a white glaze of ice lay atop everything. Kai put his arms around Gretel's waist, and they waddled like penguins through the streets, Tapioca pulling the leash in Gretel's hand.

Outside the Church of the Jesuits, whose color seemed to be blushing in the wind, they heard children singing. This church was Gret's favorite to sit in when she wanted to quiet the world around her. The interior was painted white, and crystal chandeliers hung like teardrops from a celestial place. Kai and Gretel continued toward the path to the Schloss and then began the three hundred and fifteen-stair incline. The brick retaining walls held back the mountain, ivy and moss growing old watching visitors.

"Do you believe in one moment or one decision defining a life?" Kai asked Gretel. The two often asked each other questions to which the answers were open like the night sky and numerous like the stars.

"With no doubt. I am living one with you." Gretel looked out towards the Neckar River and had a view of the Old Bridge and the start of Philosophenweg.

"Would you want to live if it brought pain to you but joy to others?" Kai tried to picture such a life. He smiled, but not lightly.

"For you I would," he answered as he imagined an alternate existence.

The ice had gotten worse on the path as the elevation increased. But the enchantment was luring, and they had nearly reached the top. Smoke from chimneys below rose upward. The town appeared to be gingerbread, like one could reach down and feast upon it. They walked towards the front of the castle. Gretel saw a young girl with her father. "Vati! Vati! You tell me I'm your princess! Now it's like we're in a fairytale!" Gretel walked closer to the edge. The Schloss wall had crumbled in the portion in front of her, leaving a drop off.

Kai, now holding Tapioca's leash, walked toward a wall where there was a better view of the mote.

Tapioca grew slightly anxious to be leaving Gretel's side, but Kai pulled her along reluctantly. "This way, junger hund. Kommen Sie dieser Weg. Come see with me."

Gretel was standing very close the edge now. She seemed mesmerized by the girl standing beside her. The girl's hair was parted to the side, some strands hanging over her eyes. The girl, not more than five, looked up at Gretel. Gret's eyes widened; it felt like she was struck with something, as if her feet had lost balance. But she was still standing. The girl looked away quickly. "Vati! Take me down there; I want to see where the fire bur—" The girl tried to turn to where her father was, but her shoe had slipped, revealing frozen stone beneath the thin layer of snow. Gretel grabbed for her hand, their palms touching like a kiss from a mother to a child. The girl pulled hard as she felt herself meeting gravity at the edge of the castle. All that lay beneath her was stone, some six hundred feet down. As Gretel used her weight to pull the girl up, her own body, like satin on skin, slipped from the frosted stone. Like lightening she fell, too quickly to scream.

"Gret."

"She's gone, she's gone. Let her go." Kai felt his father next to him, his presence somewhat scratchy, like that of the wool sweaters he used to stretch over his head as a child. He was in his father's home in the country.

"No."

His words trailed off as if they were a train pulling out of the station and rumbling down worn and rusted tracks. Then he centered himself. His words echoed themselves. Bent around and then caved in and began again. He knew where he was and that she was gone. His attention was single pointedly on her and the space in this world that she had left.

"Let her go."

The words he heard were heavy, drenched and rusted in their own way. He didn't know if his father had really spoken again, but he answered anyway.

"No. O Gretel." Kai's mouth tasted like wet stones as he tried to call for her. His father brought him warm milk with honey. The steam from the mug felt like tears evaporating from his face. His forehead was feverish in the coolness of the winter room. Nothing was real but the blanket he lay under and his father's eyes that didn't leave his side. They didn't speak much. They didn't have to. He thought he could dare not wake another day without her. The days and nights had no variation except for the color of light cast on the walls. He ate little, washed up when he had to. He thought only of ways to end his life, that which to him had lost all life. The world had become a schloss chamber reaching as far as space and time could see. Kai remained faded between restless sleeps. The memory of the descent from the Schloss had cut with an abysmal depth; it had severed a nerve, and he didn't remember finding her. Under his skin he felt slivers of glass swimming; his body a muscle, was trying to numb itself.

One night, Kai dreamt of snowflakes falling numerous and melting into him. He dreamt of finding the lake at the end of the road, chiseling away the ice, and crawling beneath it to sleep. He awoke to his father and a doctor vigorously rubbing his legs, boiling washcloths to drape on his forehead. Outside, as pale as Gretel's body in his memory, was a white field of frigid gloom with fresh tracks to and from the lake. He would wait until tomorrow. He would go again. This time more skillfully, more quietly.

Your Pants Look Baggy

Let's not freak out too quickly here,
We all have vices, Doc.
There's something in your eyes so sad.
It really is no shock.

I'm smoking, drinking, skipping work.
You're eating less I see,
And we know where such choices lead.
I hear her words — a plea.

I'm here to help in every way,
To help you get things straight.
Just let me in and you will see
I'll help you lift this weight.

You see what it is doing, right?
"The good ol' boys are back,"
I joke with her to keep things light, though
I see that I'm off track.

I've known you for a few years now,
I see that you're falling.
Can we call family to help?
Something I've been stalling...

It wants you dead, be honest here.
Did she say that out loud?

But she is right; the 'it' is me.
And I am suicidal.

Recall your days in Sheppard Pratt.
The doors locked me inside.
As I was safe behind their walls,
They forced me not to hide.

We went to group and tried to speak,
Hinged within ourselves.
I met girls struggling just like me,
Like paper dolls on shelves.

Through self-discovery and art,
I learned my voice was strong,
That I did not need vices to
Control what felt so wrong.

I could fight back with all my strength,
Grow exponentially,
Replace the paper doll I've been
With eyes that truly see

Beyond myself, into us all.
Compassion, liberate
This girl whose been confined so long,
To truly radiate.

I'll see you next week; bring your heart,
Your wisdom and your mind,
This girl that we've been searching for,
I've always known we'd find.

October Moon

The sky was peeling back
Like a cotton ball being stretched.
My stomach was cold, had been for months.
I thought of dying, of death
Coming upon me in my sleep,
So I wouldn't have to say goodbye.
I thought of sound, and how
If I had never heard his words,
I wouldn't be so sad.
How if I had never known his touch,
I wouldn't be so lonely.
And if we had never shared each other,
There'd be nothing to lose.
After I broke ground and found a place
Where no one was,
One side of me a brilliant golden light,
And on the other,
A full October moon,
Reflective in its nature.
Here I forgot about myself and saw
Things with a sliver of clarity,
Enough to warm my stomach.

Inside Out

Green tea reminds me of last winter
When we were so excited about
The size of the hills and the snow.
We'd unthinkingly take turns brewing
Each other steaming cups.
Now when I sip green tea,
The bitter taste is overwhelming,
And the thought keeps appearing in my mind,
"I don't know how I feel about anything."
I hold the cup of tea to my face
Trying to warm myself from the outside.
I think of the clay mugs we used to have
With the turquoise southwestern patterns,
How those mugs kept warm from the inside out.
And then the understanding comes
That this is how love should be.
It should move through you,
Warming you from the center outward.

Kneading My Heart

When I was married, I thought we had the same heart. Maybe that's what blinded me so much. We were young and undeveloped. Maybe my heart was spilling into his, and his mine. They were juxtaposed, but when they blended, I couldn't see my own. Now I realize I have my *own* heart. It can be empty, and I can keep it that way. Or it can be full, and I can continue to fill it. I can breathe air into it and watch it expand. I can stifle it, or mold it like dough, make bread, feed others with it. I can make it cry, make it bleed. I can make it smile, make others smile too. I can cast it into my eyes; I can talk with it, express with it, utilize it in every manner. I can change it, change the world with it. I can give it and keep it simultaneously. It can love and be loved. I can hate that it hurts, or I can rejoice that I have the ability to feel, heal, contribute, trust. It's on a journey that's never complete because there's always more work to do. There's never an end, never a ceasing to what a heart can do. It transcends lives, and we aren't for one instant without it. Its nature is intrinsic, but it can be offered to the liberation and salvation of all sentient beings. I have a heart, and I will make this life worth having one.

In Morning Practice

In morning practice change occurs in her.
And in her heart a low and thunderous purr.
The nun, she lights a lamp to offer to
Dakinis gathering in skies of blue.
And once upon a time, she read me tales
Of which they all contained a ship that sails
Across the ocean, free of ego's cling,
Where wisdom of enlightenment does ring.

The day is long, extending light with breath,
We seize the possibility of depth.
It's hard when smiles only fade away,
As if you've caught the turning down of day.
My mother gently tells me I am whole
When life unfolds, begins to take a toll.
She wraps her robes of refuge over me;
The burgundy and gold is all I see.

The Lama dancers weaving in and out
Of early memories, relieving doubt.
The Dharma teaches her to climb a hill;
The hill becomes a mountain and yet still.
Unraveling are precious jewels, all three,
Whose only purpose is to set her free.
Transmission. Longed for, searching life to life;
Renouncing, training, letting go of strife.

The circumstances giving birth somehow,
Her teacher calling, calling to come now.
"White Tara and her sangha are right here;
We must remain 'til all six realms are clear."
My hand in hers, the nun looks in my eyes,
"For lifetimes, we've had potent friendship ties.
And I will not abandon you, sweet child.
Begin anew," she told me as she smiled.

Recognizing the Ocean

I have only what I need.
I have a conch shell where the roaring
Of the ocean is always heard.
The sound reminds me to offer
The indestructible Dharma
To worlds that are intangible to me,
Where some good from hearing a sound
Outside samsara's poisons might occur.

I have a heart in which every day
I pray will remain open,
Even through the pain and suffering I see.
I pray it opens until there are no boundaries
Between my heart and your suffering.
I pray, even though I have only what I need,
That I can give you all you've ever wanted.

Free Spirit

I strip down to my underwear and
Glance in the mirror at a paper doll.
I put on the black polka dot dress
That slips like sex on my skin.
I think about last night and how
I fell asleep watching a movie so depressing
That even my dreams were heavy,
And when I woke up, I was let down by life.
So now I stare in the mirror as if
Staring into his eyes, back when
I couldn't fill him up enough
With whatever he wanted.
And I was left feeling like a child
Who had displeased her parents again.
Expectations—it's what causes us to think
That other falls short.
I try to stay deeply humbled
By the weight we all carry — each other.
I study the shape of eyes;
They tell me truth and intention.
Begin within, begin within.
It's a mantra in my head,
But maybe my misunderstanding
Keeps me from ever reaching out,
From ever breaking this boundary
That ties my wrists and strangles my tongue.
You, me, this energy exchange which is like

A handshake every time we meet.
One time I let myself fall into his arms;
It was like tripping
Into a place I'd been
But hadn't been in a long time.
I stood there until it didn't feel right and then let go
And left quickly and never went back.
But I think about it often, when I let myself.
When I'm brave enough.
When I cut my wrists free.
My words sometimes come out
Tripping over each other
Like kids that don't know any better.
Rough housing and romping in freedom.
Surprising even me.
I only wish my whole being could do the same.

Topanga Canyon

I didn't know the road would end at the ocean,
although the map showed it so. All its beauty rushing
down the canyon walls, spilling recklessly into a
torrent of salt and rock. It was where celebrities went
to hide out and lounge privately; where hippies marked
their mural-painted buses, losing articles of clothing as
they ran, feet slipping in sand, into the water; where
teenage boys ditched school to play volleyball with the
wind. We were an entanglement of all three, leaving
college in Arizona, taking to the road over the golden
hills until we reached the ocean. We were young and
elegant and hiding from a world that wanted us to be a
certain way.

About halfway down the canyon, we had stopped to
get coffee at a little store built into the trees. We
stocked up on camping supplies, mainly chocolate bars
and graham crackers, and firewood too. We hadn't
camped much on this trip, maybe twice. Our daughters
were with us, Della being only two months old. We
had taken Asia camping for the first time when she
was six weeks old, because nothing could keep us out
of the woods.

As I write this now, reflecting back, it's been nearly
four years since our last camping trip in California. If
you would have told me then that it would be our last

night camping together, my tears would have swum
out, saying let's never leave, this moment, this canyon.
Let the beauty rush down and the undertow bite. Let
the storms roll in and out, the tide, the changing moon.
Let the rocks change to sand, and from coarse to
smooth. But let's never leave. Let us grow into the
canyon, like the trees into the store. We'd grow up,
learn how to be adults somehow. Our love would go
from high school sweethearts, fiery and new, to
established and mature. But our spirit would stay the
same, an echo in a winding canyon overlooking a wild
ocean.

Quickening

I kiss her happy birthday and
Clench my jaw to drown my tears
That naturally recognize how quickly
Five years makes her grow.
I turn the doorknob to leave and
The warmth of my belly becomes significant.
I feel her birth resonate in me.
Unthinkingly I glance at the clock and
My eyes widen so slightly that
None of the children in the room notice.
6:50 a.m. exactly.
As I leave the room, I am aware that
Every doorway I walk through is a lotus opening.

Heart in Corset

I accept my fucked up, sloppily stitched,
Broken black heart.
There's no exploding sky above
Meaningless cupid arrows.
I can't paint a smile in fuchsia on hopelessness.
I bend 'in love' out of love like a gymnast
Until everything appears to be lacking something,
And at the time it's the only thing I want,
Because I swear it is the one thing
That will heal black hearts.
I'm a modest girl that has somehow been entrenched
In self-hatred, as I hold everyone else up.
We're all torn between delusional
Righteousness and self-pitying thoughts.
It's black, it's black, I light a match
And it's a mourning gray over easy.
And at the end of life they'll stutter,
"She was, she was… She could have been…"
The hunger pains draw me in like a corset
That's laced up my back in loops
Forming teardrop bows.
Traces are left on my body just as jet streams
Are constant in an effortlessly changing sky.
I painted it on canvas so I could see it as still life,
So I could briefly stop chasing it.
Then I tore it to shreds so I could hear
The sounds of fibers coming untwined.

Now the sky cries acrylics towards the north region;
The splatter technique splashes against my ribcage,
Soaking my black heart with color.

In Seam

Girls should be seamless.
I had *thought* that once.
But isn't it freeing
To know we're not?

X

My day is his night.
It's like slanted etches on scrap paper,
Never crossing to form an x.
There's no here I can depend on.
It's like missing the last train on a cold night
When your breath is white.
It's losing possibility,
Friendship in words
And nothing else.
Like a blind person drawing a picture
Of what he's thinking.
It's not having the time you need to make
A sound decision, so you rush and settle
And nothing else.
It's gaining insight but having no one
To tell so you cry into a pillow
And then sleep.
And the sleep makes you numb
And the blanket breathes for you,
And you lie without life,
Away from the cold air and thoughts,
Where neither can find you,
Where it doesn't matter
That his day is my night.

The Curve of a Cobblestone Street

He heard bombs when the train doors slammed,
And the French woman looked at him
As if he'd caused the war.
Paris was nothing more than dry wine from bottleneck,
Bread from a basket to settle my stomach,
And the heated breath
Of a French boy in the metro tunnel.
It was not much more than the view of the Pantheon
Slouched at the top of
Le Montagne Sainte-Genevieve,
The lighting of Gauloises,
And a street lined with a butchery,
A bakery, and a flower shop.

It was more than me catching my breath in his hands,
And him whispering to me
What no one had said in months.
Paris was a cold room through the courtyard,
Us entangled in itchy blankets,
And a skull key with grooves
That wouldn't unlock the door.
It was a sink in the room, a toilet across the garden,
And two Euros for a shower. Paris was trying to taste
The difference in their fries while waiting for the next
And only train-hopping path
To get us back to Germany.

We smoked like the French, drank from the bottle,
Called ourselves stupid fucking Americans
At least thirty times
As we tripped over our lost luggage
And inability to find our way
In the city of romance.
It wasn't the Eiffel Tower or Mona Lisa
Or impressionistic art
Or anything I thought it would be.
It wasn't a café on a street corner, people-watching
While blowing milky steam from a teacup.
It did, however, consist of the best chocolate croissant.

Paris was watching a cat climb
From a bread basket in the train station.
It was tiny cups of coffee
That were only filled halfway.
It was finding a cathedral and being moved to tears
Simply from the light coming through
The stained glass windows.
My Paris was before I understood
His need to be embraced.
It was finding happiness in a complete mess
And laughing until it hurt.
Paris was a glimmer of a city above graffitied walls
As the train wailed and screeched
And pulled us from her view.

Buttresses Don't Fall

Don't fall.
Don't fall.
Rest, spin.
"Talk to me, just talk to me.
Don't fall asleep."
And then he says my name
And I am awake because —
Never trust a man
Who whispers your name.

But despite, he satisfies me,
Finally, I'm full.
I haven't thought about dying.
I haven't cried,
And no one's asked what's wrong.

Come on, Laura,
Don't fall.
Earlier today, he had met me
In the nave of a cathedral,
And it was my favorite structure thus far,
Because it was white and appeared weightless,
Like his pale lips that blow steam
That dissolve my frown.

No, no, I'm not falling.
He traces my arm, I shudder, he whispers.

He says my breathing was all off.
I remember dreaming of falling,
My body jolted awake.
He takes me, holding me closer,
Until I fall asleep again.

And then he fell too,
And we both slept,
Window to our room slightly cracked,
Red roofs pouring over the mountainside,
The castle ready to tumble
To our doorstep to tell us
Fairytales are real.

Make of Me Disquiet

He first touched me in the darkroom
When the negatives were just being exposed
To the photo paper.
Then he left his marks on my inner thighs
So that all I could think was how tender this life is.
When I exited the room
And looked at the barren treetops,
I saw static, but the electricity was in me,
Once again like bleeding purple ink,
Staining and forming pools of delicate bruises.
The front yard lay soggy with patches of snow
That sat like icebergs in deep blue water.
The outside radiated the color of an eggplant's skin.
Sky reached out restlessly, provoked —
And the snow began to fall,
Cooling the hot places on my body.
The snowflakes melted into my cream skin, filling me
With the scent of Earl Grey tea and wet earth.
And then the way beer warms my stomach
And then my hands,
My face became flushed with warmth,
The qualm slowly fading,
Leaving nothing gentle in its wake.

My Self-Conscious Girl

He called me this after sweet sex unthawed
On a blizzard-adorned day off from work
When I snuck past him to the clear cascade
Of water drizzling behind the curtain hung
To hide our bodies from the outside world.
While normally the bedroom isn't lit,
Today it was as bright as snow and I
Pretended not to know, our figures laid
Out on the heat-soaked sheets like linear hills.
Am I defined by what I do not do?
Who should I blame for this self-conscious girl?
Is she my own creation like some kind
Of Frankenstein, a sloppily stitched up doll?
Or is it that I've always been this way?
My tendency is to hide, to shy, to press
Myself against the outer wall of a room
So I will go unnoticed. I'm no more
Than a girl who's followed by a brilliant
Poised adjective. I'm his self-conscious girl,
Wrapped in a towel and under sheets with blinds
Pulled closed, beside the snowy streets lit by
The moon who's paler than my snowy skin.
I'll dream of anything but what I'm not.

No Compliment

It's grey, it's grey, it's pouring over easy.
I'm breathing in the clouds and choking down
The stormy water, troubled and uneasy.
I force myself to contemplate the drown.

The way depression folds you, folds you in
And in and in until there is no out.
I'd rip it off if I had any skin,
Or reach out if I were not hushed by doubt.

Someone disrupts me writing this to say
My eyes are stormy grey. He hasn't read
This, but he sees the weather giving way,
My eyes a tousled silver in the sky.

Was said before the day when I was born
That always I'd be happy or forlorn.

Johnny

A man once called me Dapple,
And I was his morning dew.
I was his drop of dew, dawning
In the vibrant light.
He called me Dapple,
And I was his girl next door.
A man that called me Dapple
Claims I saved his life.
He revealed himself to me,
And we would laugh for hours.
A man once called me Dapple,
And now I've never been so alone.
I was the girl next door,
But did he ever really know?
Every day we'd pass the time
Saving each other's lives.
He would tell me the sunlight
Touched this plant at a specific angle,
At a distinct hour, and every morning
He rose to look at the dew sparkle, glisten.
A man once called me Dapple,
But I don't think he ever knew
What that word meant.

Storm Cloud

She's his little storm cloud.
He takes her into his embrace and squeezes
Until she breaks into sheets of rain
That white out the summer air.
Passive bouts of longing, gentle eyes giving
And stripping him down to bare skin.
All moist with dew, he takes her into his arms
That reach around her with ease.
He mistakes her smallness for fragility,
And as she sits on his bed, tears smearing makeup,
Laughter to make light the sound of her thunder,
She strikes out with what she knows not is lightning.
She's unable to control the downpour of emotions,
And he's simply wishing it away,
Because he wants her rain,
Torrential yet quiet, all to himself.

His Aftershock

Afterwards, the pain from inside seeped out
A tender pinkish red onto the tissue paper.
He is not the first man to tell me
How fragile and delicate I seem.
Now I was starting to know what they all meant.
Afterwards, I am broken into
Small parts, slightly listless,
Hushed and reflective, painfully
Aware of being separate,
And having a soft world of secrets inside me,
Secrets like mazes that enter
As pathways into my mind.
And I wonder if everyone has this
Secret world inside them.
Maybe these are the roads that bleed.
Maybe it's not just me who feels
Stripped and broken into,
Or like a sponge that simply can't help but absorb.
I stand in the bathroom and let my eyes,
Like a cascading waterfall, drift down my body.
Breasts, navel, legs. All are shaking
From the aftershock of an internal earthquake.
But I can't tell the starting point,
Where the earth inside me began to crack.
It could have been many places, many secrets.

Accepting the sorrow, I think, "I cannot heal
That which I don't know the origin of."
And though I try, it's like trying to hem
The edges of a blanket that has no middle.

Empty Space

Instead of bringing a couch
Into my living room
To fill floor space,
I bring boys.
The pictures aren't even hung yet.
Instead it's blank walls,
And no flowers on the dining table.
But instead, empty beer bottles,
Sticky shot glasses.
I give myself away,
Because I'm scared to face
A sea of pain that is waiting
When no one is around.
And when I'm alone I blast
Music so loud I lose perception
And become enveloped in the space,
The space between a hand
And the strings of a guitar,
Between the palm
And the head of a drum.
If played just right,
The boys become instruments.
And I feel like the wind blown
From the mouth of a flautist,
Though I take no credit
For the music they make.

Boys Like Sandpaper

They know how to break me,
How to smash me,
How to smooth me
How they want me.
All I want to do is break away.
They know how to say one word
And as it ripples,
It's a constant reminder
That they see women as objects.
They fire in the kiln
What was never meant to be.
Deairing, reshaping, burnishing,
And finally sintering.
I don't need to be worked or handled,
Pressed or glazed.
I am not a finished product,
Nor do I require assembly.
I am nobody's piece of pottery.

Never Again

I wake up with a bruise on my wrist,
Feeling full of something I don't want to be,
Having talked about things I didn't want to release.
I forgot who I am, a pattern
That has become too familiar.
I sip coffee the color of his pants,
Pull his shirt from my ribcage and,
In an effort to forget what we did,
I strip my bed of its blankets and sheets,
Placing them on a rigorous cycle
And watching them spin
Through the pane of glass on the front of the washer.
I am wishing my own self to be cleansed the same.
And later, when I climb into bed at night, new sheets
Turned down, my skin showered, my mind bathed,
I once again make the promise: Never again.

An Untitled Sunday

I turn the heat up in my house,
My body aching and walked through,
And I want nothing more
But the chill to be gone
And to sleep in unknowing.

The Sadness of Sea Glass

I was fractured long
Ago, though my edges have
Smoothed and I appear
Whole again. But you should know,
There was always more to me.

Waking From Slumber

I fall asleep in my confusion, and when I awake,
It's raining all around me.
I dreamt I was drumming on his stomach,
Drumming a freedom beat, drumming into him heat.
It was the opposite of what I feel,
That I actually had something to offer
In my slumber, the ebb of this
Connection was licking the earth,
Like the salty ocean lapping upon the coast.
In the rain I smell the distant ocean.
The wind is moving the rain
In a way that makes it slam
Against the glass doors that I'm looking out.
Through the grayness in the sky, I see
My reflection in each and every raindrop,
Falling quickly, becoming part of the earth
In this cleanse that's taking place.
Erased is my name and my body,
Words that I've spoken and those that I have not.
I throw myself out the window of perception.
Here, giving rise to the Bodhicitta,
Where all thoughts and duality dissolve.

Finding My Sight

Darkness is much of the months I've been trudging myself through, moving in wrong directions on repeat, a harmful autopilot. Darkness was knowing but doing nothing. Darkness was being drunk in her garage, where even my anxiety was incoherent. Darkness was waking in the middle of the night, dehydrated, choking on fear, on faults, on decisions, choking on everything but water. It was being in a cell of loneliness and withdrawal and holding the key to unlock the cell in my hand, but being too blind to see it and too shaky to use it even if I could see it.

There is no darkness when I am in urdhva hastasana and then fold my praying mantis limbs, hands to heart. The darkness is not present when I drink water, and like rain gently drumming ground, consciously make a prayer to purify my body, speech, and mind. I'm finding comfort and clarity in a cup of tea and leaving boredom in the bottle. I'm giving up on going to the dark to try and find light. The less I try to hide my anxiety and fear in darkness, the more light comes through my stained-glass eyes, shining colors in and all around me, colors that I could not see before.

Flooding

The flooding stopped, and I watched
The water drain away while the sun
Shone down on me
And made my skin shimmer.
Like diamonds, I saw the future
Lying upon wet black asphalt.
I took my umbrella down
And the last cloud hovering
Above my head washed
Away the dirt in my mind.

Karma Exhausted

I look into a beaded mala, see
One hundred eight faces, and clasp my palms
Around the beads and pray, perhaps a plea.

Perhaps I still have yet to learn what calms
The mind and how to pray with an open heart.
I hear my rib cage giving in with qualms,

The way a lung sounds punctured, torn apart.
I beg, as children do, to her Supreme
Awakened Mother, a face of truth as art,

Of lotuses in bloom, a rising beam
In a stilled and silent lake. I swim out to
The center of this lake, and blue beads stream

Off skin. I climb on lotus land, subdue
The part of me that's given up, this karmic
Weight that's gathered in a heavy dew.

I strip the suffering, admit I'm sick
With ego's cling. I pray to find a cure,
To clear the haze that has become so thick.

Natal Signs

He said, "You're flying and I know,"
Like saying *Namaste*. He said the glow
Was purple, pale and light the day we graced,
The stars hydrangeas, bunched and hanging low.

If there were centers of the heart, then laced
with thought and universe, perhaps we'd taste
The sweetness, sameness moving ever slow
Through each of us. It waits to be embraced.

The sun is Leo as it should, all fiery and bold,
The moon is where her sadness grows, consoled,
No never, swimming there in Pisces spaced
With dreams and intuition, loves untold,

The moon has quiet ways and intrigue sewn
Though seldom is this seen, like finding gold.
The moon must ask the sun to step
Dethrone

Before the sulk can fully settle. She's
In awe of moon dust wandering slow with ease.
She takes her time with reservation, strewn
Across the galaxy, the Venus tease

For Virgo yearns for nondescript appeal.
So take her dancing, Silver Love, and she'll
Pull down hydrangeas from the stars and seize
The hidden lunar kiss that's now revealed.

The Ones

She takes my hand as if it's my heart,
Her skin a lotus petal warmed by the sun.
She takes my hand and with her
We enter her alter room.
Cloaked in gold, her mandala.
We are treasure seekers.
We have entered caves, diligently,
We have prayed and unearthed,
Finding it's not tangible
Is a blessing in itself,
For there is nothing to gain from the outside
When the treasure rests within.
She vowed that when she found us,
She would pull us in.
Her return again fulfills the vow.
In meeting us, she begins the journey.
We have forgotten, but she recognizes us.
She says
We are the ones.
We are all the ones.

Condensation

It's noon on Saturday, and the air is made of rain
today. My mind is quiet, and the soggy street is not.
My mother is at yard sales and calls me five times in
one hour to tell me what she's found. And every time I
take a breath instead of screaming, but my mind is not
so quiet anymore. Tomorrow's Sunday, and my father
will have erased me from where he 'penciled' me in on
his calendar, because I am his disposable daughter.
The next day will be Monday, and work will roll in
like the cycling of the daily newspaper. The kids aren't
here, so I light up a cigarette, sit on the wood beams,
read Kerouac and Ginsberg, and try to find Buddhism
in lines of streams of consciousness. I decide I don't
like Ginsberg because of the way he treated his
mother. His words become hard for me to read. But
then my mother calls again, this time about the yard
sale on Ancient Oaks, and maybe I can read Ginsberg
a little more. I light up another cigarette, because what
the hell? The kids aren't here. The writers seem
Buddhist in the sense that they let the thoughts come in
and go out without clinging but trusting that the
meaning will find itself and someone will understand it
down the road, because we are all made of human
nature, and our roads are bound to cross at some time.

I can't concentrate on what's in front of me
because I'm stuck in a writing mind, and I curse
Natalie Goldberg for teaching me to unrein writing

146

mind, which has kept me leashed and captivated for years. In her workshop, we had practiced walking meditation, and in all my years I had never done this and struggled to walk slow enough in the gardens of Sedona where we wandered, some of us like zombies, some tree huggers, some 'touching peace'. Maybe the role of Buddhism in their writing was the stripping down to bare mind, deconstructing poetic form, saying fuck it and just writing, however unconventional it seemed.

I'm dizzy from the world, from the constant traffic off my balcony through the trees that are turning so slowly this year. I focus on the one flower below and the one bumblebee that lands on the flower. I focus on the one mind we all share and perhaps find a sliver of peace I can rest on. My father calls, and the one thing I hear is the ending of the phone call when he says, "I love you." It's louder than all the words he just said, but I wonder if it's just my perception or if he really meant it that way.

I believe my mind is made of rain today, a thick rain made of sheets, but it hasn't broken from the clouds just yet. The lump in my throat is condensation building, words that I keep inside, muting myself like I always have. The tension in my chest is thunder rolling in the distance, and the storm is imminent, in me *and* outside my window.

I used to be scared of storms. I'd cover my ears tightly, so that all sounds were muffled. I'd cry and make my mother pull the car over so the pounding of raindrops on the windshield was not so loud. I was scared of how loud the world could be. I wanted softness but rarely found it. I retreated within where I could keep things quiet. The air thickens like the lining of a woman's inner body, the cycle building once again. I open windows up, because you know I love the fumes of dirty America.

My aunt calls me just to tell me that smiling reduces stress. "So smile!" she says.

My stomach is churning, but I think it's just my mind turning poem into more than just poem. I reread O'Hara's *Why I Am Not a Painter* because it makes me laugh. And my stomach isn't so tight. Maybe I won't starve myself tonight, and maybe I can be okay with figure and form and imperfection and free verse. Full of what it is, nothing more or less, simply uncontrived. I hope to be a poem someday. I would be confessional and raw, not blank or masked or claiming to embody anything more than simply what I am. Whose smiles come like rain only less predictable, whose fears and anxieties present themselves in everyday life, because I am human, and I can't hide that.

Crab Apples

The crab apples beneath my steps
Are bursting with redness
The same color as my face
When I talk to you.
I see the word 'chasing'
Scribbled on a piece of paper in a box and
My thoughts are chasing my emotions
And my emotions chasing my thoughts.
The day feels dehydrated without you,
It's still fruitful, but not the same.
And I wonder how long I can stand here
Without bringing this fruit to my lips,
Knowing its sweetness is mixed with bitterness.
I take a bite and think of bringing bushels home,
But my stomach starts to turn thinking about it.
So I just stand there a little while longer,
Feeling the bitterness beneath my shoes,
And trying so hard to extract the sweetness.

Shoreline

Her early summer feet burn on the sand,
Though on this Saturday, it's early still.
The muffled wind is rippling, trying to hush
The ocean's uproar, hush the current's pulse.
And on this day, she sees that she can push
Her emotions to the back of her mind, leaving
Her face to be distant, quiet, not distraught.
She casts her gaze to sea and leaves it there.
And all she feels are rays and the bite of the salt
On her skin. It's wet, then dries, then tightens in
And her emotions tighten and burn beneath
Her bronzing skin, a tender pinkish-gold.
And if she were to petrify this way,
Absorbed in blank expression, she would dry,
Allowing little weathering to rouse
The moisture-less land beneath her skin's facade.
She may become parched beached wood, worn —
Yet still the same as she always was in substance.
And so she chooses softening instead
Of hardening, although she doesn't know where
She may end up, like how she doesn't know
What the seagull sees when he dives face first
Into tossing waters.

Sea Glass and Stones

I found you barefoot and brumal;
I was as cold as you.
Your heart stone, mine shattered glass.
Maybe hope was blazoned in sky's silver before rain.
I would fall if I were standing now,
But I am already on my knees.
I know you from before,
But I don't know who I was or where we were.
I am more curious to know who you were,
Because I know that I was me.
When we found one another, we were in the sea,
Not yet smoothed by water's sharp pull,
By water's fluent being.
We know sea glass is formed with time,
But seldom do we think of each one's history.
That once it was something else,
And that the something never leaves.
Doubtful, but maybe eventually I will understand.
Most likely I'll just see glimmers through hues
Of polished glass and stone.

Todo Para Todo

The sky smells like pepper, speckled
Black and white, flavoring us moonlight and stars.
I stay up with you all night, hear all the words you say.
There's background noise heard from your room
Of the shuffling soldiers in the barracks,
Leaving for missions and duties at all hours.
Outside the world around us promotes fear,
And that flame is in me, I know.
Before we had spent too many nights here,
I told you I was already sad for when this ends,
Tragedy always lingering
Like words that won't leave my tongue.
Maybe it's just my own world promoting fear in me.

In Puerto Rico you broke me open
Like the top of a coco frio;
You said you found sweet milk
That you knew was there.
I begged you to take me to Old San Juan,
And there we bought poetry from shops
And found poetry on walls, 'Life is a metaphor.
Love is not a metaphor'.
I had looked back at you with the camera over my eye,
Whispered, and I don't know if you heard,
"Love is a metaphor we don't want to believe."

I could abandon tragedy,

Like a rag doll left in the worn-stone street,
If only I could remember
The salsa-stepped coastline of Fajardo
Or how I knew you were for me
When you told me Shakespeare
Tastes like Holland waffles.
Instead I put you in my current,
Where you even took the time
To ask me how to navigate.
But the sea has no pattern to its mesopic tone.
Lo siento, lo siento.

Your palm is on my forehead,
And I'm wrapped in your arms.
You're holding me closer,
And you're making more sense,
But it's making less sense to me.
I smile and frown as I push
The softest place in my life away.
Our eyes are damp and softened
As we fall asleep in tangles.

I wake up, but I'm still sleeping and rip myself away,
Stretching my t-shirt over my head, down my ribcage,
"Can't love, can't hurt."
I dream with no words again and when I awake
All I remember is patience in dream form.
But I'm still not ready to give you Sunday mornings,
So I leave quickly, head rushing like the waterfalls

Of El Yunque. As I drive I cry porcelain
Into my lap, because I can't change and I can't love,
And it's no secret now.
Down the road the creek bed is still breathing fog,
And the yellowing fields of soy are outstretched
Like another hopeless fall.

Later you call me. "I had a dream I couldn't find you.
You were sad
And went away. And when I woke you were gone."
The long pause reaches upward
Like mountains before you speak again,
"Remember that song I translated for you
After kayaking the bio bay?

"Our love rumbles,
And I love you, todo para todo."

Blush

We're kissing over soft-serve frozen cream
And later we'll pull turtlenecks, fake sass
Undressing, window yawning. Autumn dream
Is sneaking in through wavy bubble glass.

Our sentiment turns the room a pumpkin-spice.
The city flickers, glazes gusty eyes
Because I'm well enough to be enticed
By harvest's plumping moon as it gives rise.

Remember me by pulling fruit from trees
In autumn's orchards, golden, dappled boughs
That drop their crumbled blush before the freeze.
The window's slight that nature's time allows.

Before, you knew the taste of the apples' round
Appearance, knowing shortened life is fate.
In equal giving, sweet outliving, we found
Each other. Place your hand here. Feel heart rate.

Simple

I pretend to smile but I'm crying.
I'm crying because I'm happy, but I can't be
Because I'm sad.
You drive south to see me.
We're wearing the same shirt.
We fall asleep together.
I cut your hair.
We hold each other.
It's simple.
We forget. We remember. We forget.
It's time for you to go.
We kiss and kiss and kiss.
And we don't let go.

Winter Blankets

Part 1

The time together feels short when it stops in a hospital. And the bedroom was left smelling like lethargy, the color of bluntness and confusion. Our last conversations were abstract words only tracing real thoughts. And then you left in the moonlight that had forgotten it was already morning. You left with a kiss that had been freshly showered and uniformed. I didn't grab your arm and tell you to stay like other mornings. I didn't kiss back. I shifted in the winter blankets, and that was it. I am colder than winter sometimes. I am worse than lying naked on stone. I leave creviced earth, tarred and blackened by eruptions. I plan my own evacuation route and someday I know I'll leave.

Part 2

What little leaves are left in me are shivering on this tree. I feed the birds sunlight and seeds. "Wake up!" It's winter and they need to eat. I throw it into the wind and watch it fall into grass and soil. I breathe out the painful gasps into my palms, my fingers already twigs, my hands already helpless. And I am hopeless in the fading evolution of humankind. And you ask me why I cry, and they ask me why I think of leaving so often. I can't answer but I know the answer. I can't give, but I know the gift. I can't love, but I know the effort. I'm a white oak with no leaves; I'm a tree with no bark; I'm a heart with no beat. It's a love with no last. Children cry in their honesty because they don't deny the suffering, that the world hurts when you come in. It hurts as you grow old. It hurts as you die and then prepare to do again. And then there is the constant resistance; heart bursting out, skin holding in, eyes revolving doorways. Doorways you can't lock, I've tried. It's the way our blood has no feeling when it's pouring out, but our nerves scream, and tissues fight to close the gap.

Part 3

Tonight, I'm in Rudy's gravel lot, parked where the gas pumps used to be, back when it was a working station. You tell me to look at the moon, so I do. The edges are torn and it's far away. You tell me the distance from me to the moon is how much you love me. You tell me you miss me, naked in your bed, when it's dark and your eyes are adjusting, and the softness and warmness of skin as the moon comes through the window—that is what you miss. I turn on a track like a marble rolling down chutes with a gradual decline. I wait for this mood to dissolve, ice thawing to slush; I'll be a puddle again. I'll be the tears we haven't yet cried.

Part 4

Feels so cold. Clouds like a front, a wall in the sky. I dream of ghosts, of funerals, of meeting you, of a chance encounter, of being raised, of being born, of never being born, of facades, of collages of ideas. I dream of dreams, only dreams. That's all these moments are. That's all they ever were. I can't sleep tonight; I just keep listening to the rain. I just keep feeling the downpour in me. It's cold without you here. Perhaps winter is housed in all of us, like the cycling of seasons, the tide, the moon. Maybe I'm not all winter after all. Maybe I'm not as frozen as I thought and thawing is not as hard, is not as distant or undoable as I had conceived. Next time I see you, I show you the moon's terminator line. I tell you that you must see it up close, the fading of the sun's light or the illumination of the moon's darkness. I don't know which one anymore. All I know though, is that the moon is far away, and you love me an awful lot.

My Cupid

My heart paper thin,
He blew me a breezy kiss,
And I blew away.

Diamonds When I Cry

I passed the gems at Tiffany's again
And started thinking what I hadn't said.
The quiet moments in the car I shed
The soft, blue sobs that glint as they descend,
The way a slip falls down one's back and then
One's breasts, one's waist, one's feet.
Most tears, unsaid.
You saw the slip cascade from me in bed
And maybe holding wine I looked softened,
The stem between my fingers. Only then
I saw the fingerprinted glass, the dread
That this is what I leave on you instead
Of love that shimmers from a treasured friend.
And your proposal? Worthy of the end.
You might as well have thrown the ring, embed
My worth to you. Asked me bare skin to wed...
I wasn't even decent. "Try again,"

Is what I said, which came long after, "I
Just can't, I can't," between so many gasps.
Tomorrow waits like origami now,
The creases made, and maybe you'll retry
In moonlight on a walk once there's a lapse
In time. Or we may never make that vow.
In solitude, I think of why, of how
You may have never had the chance. Perhaps
No quiet moment came; I know I cry

What seems like all the time, and I avow.
The box was turquoise blue, then come the gaps.
And I'm okay with that, but not with why.

Sonnet to Susanna

"Breathless, we flung us on a windy hill, Laughed in
the sun, and kissed the lovely grass." Rupert Brooke

The lacy lights above our heads turn on
Just after dusk, just after we say I do.
We dance the rumba to our chosen song.
You fling the garter, stitched with my something blue.
The braided arch built by my father's hands
Stands proud, adorned with flowers, by the lake.
Exotic trees and shrubs embellish the land.
You hold me close, and I taste the almond cake
Between us, lips pressing, the way we're pressed
For one another, and especially this day,
When all our plans have taken form. I'm dressed
In white and you in gray, our love on display.
Tomorrow what will we remember most?
The allurement of Susanna Farm, our host.

Growing a Quenepa Tree

After I sucked the stringy fruit from the seeds,
I cloaked them carefully in a moist napkin
And snuck them through the customs gate. The deed
Was done. We hopped on the plane,
My seeds wrapped in my bag,
Securely leaving island life.
Arriving home, I coddled them in pots
Until they sprouted roots, ones that enticed
My dreams of growing paradise. Love knots
That formed beneath the soil's surface sprout
In green that bursts to the sun. My Spanish limes,
My babies with more seed than fruit, reach out
Further from sugarcane valleys that climb
Away from roadside stops, where for just two
Dollars I stole a Zion you grew into.

Pillar of Life

She's four, but if you knew her
You'd know she's lived outside her age.

She'll ask you how you are
And really care to know

She'll tell you to turn the air off in the car
On a hot day because she wants
To feel the sun rays on her face.
On a cold day she says she doesn't feel the chill,
Because she's learned to tune it out.

When she holds her sister's hand and my hand,
She says we are a caterpillar,
Our auras meshing, three into one.

She'll tell you the bowl on our dining table
That is filled with rice is a reminder
Of what many children have to eat in a whole day.

She's a girl who, after surgery,
Asked me to pray for her all night by her bedside,
I sang in her ear as she hung onto her life force
Through the pain in her belly and then in her chest.

She's the one who was up two days after
Surgery peddling a tricycle through the halls

And four days after surgery running to the stupa
To make prayers for a long life.
She is determined, and I believe in her life
And what she gives the world.

She prays to Amitabha, Buddha
Of Infinite Light and Life,
In half lotus posture, dedicating her prayers
To the liberation and salvation of all sentient beings.

Little Conquistador

She throws her fist up to the sky declaring
An exploration, taking the statue's stance.
The Caribbean roars beyond the walls,
Splashing its salty sting against El Morro.
Ponce de Leon points her onward. "Search!
For there is always something to discover,"
I can almost hear him whispering to her.
She contrasts with the white cathedral wall,
The Spanish architecture with island flare.
As if she's walking on a canvas — blank,
Her fanciful brushwork paints a naïve
Art form that's neither concrete nor surreal.
She's basking in *tabula rasa*, youth,
A fountain all her own, not yet diluted.
I never want her to believe that all
Has been discovered, seen, and understood.
Perhaps, though, all of us are painting life
In fugitive colors destined to fade.

Night Run

I swipe the cards and rush down the stairs,
Already feeling the steam that's seeped out.
We push the white-glazed door open
And choose a locker.
And then I hurry them with the other
Herd of parents to the pool.
The steam is thick now, making it hard to breathe.
Sometimes I sit in here for the hour,
Remembering when I used to sit in the steam room
At Los Abrigados, remembering so much more.
Today I walk back through the locker room,
Abandoned now.
I go up the stairs and into the night.
My familiar shoes are on, my friends,
And they carve to my feet.
I start off under the streetlamps, running,
Whatever pace my shoes take me.
The pavement underneath sends shocks
Up my body; they're subtle but loud.
I take the road to the right, though it's so dark,
I question my choice, but not enough to turn around.
There is a moment before breaking a sweat.
The body becomes tingling fire,
There's a pressure rising.
And then there's no choice but to sweat,
Like condensation forming on a cool glass,
When all the heat is outside, only, in reverse.

I run until that heat is gone,
Until there's nothing left but the tingling, no fire.
I run until the hour's up, until I have to go back
To meet my children at the pool's edge,
To wrap them in towels and take them home.

Utopian June

I sat out on the deck and wished for June.
In the spell of time's pale glare, I am aware
Of the absent roar, a feeling I've aged too soon.
At fourteen-and-a-half we would declare
Sun Days. We'd drag through grass a folding chair
For each of us, rub coconut on skin,
Then beg the sun to strike like rain on tin.

I always knew the roar was strongest then,
That there would never be another time
When we, like wildflowers grew, formed stems,
Sprouts of small buds, then blooms of peerless prime.
Our freedom was unrivaled, so sublime.
Yet down the street, the school sat like a shell
Without the youthful roars and daily bell.

Sunday Games

I watch the game in cooling autumn air.
The trees envelop us, dropping their leaves
With timeless beauty. Caught in the golden glare
Of the weekend sun, this girl, my girl, now weaves

The field. My eyes stay on my daughter, she
Who fascinates me with her confidence,
While I'm adorned with insecurities.
She traces the trees with gleaming innocence.

Later the kids all gather in the streets
For what they call The Berry Wars, wherein
They fill their fists with red and choose their teams
And run until the weakened sun gives in.

Today Doesn't Have a Name

I'm waiting for my appointment to begin.
In the next room over, a woman's being told
"Four centimeters dilated," while I'm
About to be unnaturally dug in
Before I walk into the autumn gold.
I'll clutch my uterus and wait for pulse

As if as if as if the baby's there.
Outside and overcast, it's blown away,
The wish to conceive without the IUD.
Like leaves ripped from the stems, orphaned, skating
Wide streets. But my street, small, has a rake that tears
Each seed from ground and keeps them all at bay.
I wasn't ever good at dilating.

The Rustle in Calm

I'm raking leaves,
Reflecting sky,
Late in day.

This quiet moment
Of coming together
After being apart.

In the raking
Of leaves, I push back
The sea with a hush.

I push leaves
To the bare wood's edge
Where deer roam in morning fog.

Only sometimes I'm
Awake to witness the fog's
Ebb before it fades.

Ode to 'Changing Color'

The gallery with crooked floors cradles the one
I've come to see, the feminine auburn leaves.
The Eeyore-colored clouds curtail the sun
Into hibernation, the way a woman grieves.
The painting mimics what I try to stow
Away, the secret loss, the unborn cry.
I leave the studio, emotions swell
A rain-soaked ground. I drive a country road.
A sunflower-tinted sunset paints the sky
Above a town built around a wishing well.

Tossed in Change

You hungry yet? He nods his head,
And so we plan to grab a sandwich
After we leave the hospital, after
We find out if I've miscarried.
We're more confused than early fall
And now it's late November. All
The leaves have almost blown away
As we both brace ourselves for winter
And maybe a separation.
What I remember most from last
Week at the cabin were the knots
In pine walls and the feel of the quilt
Around my arms, the heaviness
Of cloth upon my shoulders and
The way my head hung lower when
I stumbled down the crooked stairs;
The smell of pumpkin pie-fill as
I poured it in the flaky crust;
The rusted metal box of change
(For spices used) that hung on the wall.
And I remember the way the change
Had sounded clashing against the sides
As I tossed it in for the cinnamon.
Hollow, the way my thoughts can sound
When I can't get them to slow and soon
They're tossed aside, discarded, leaving
No visible impact on me.

Change feels different when you think
Of it, rather than when you are
Immersed in it. Sometimes it's less
Scary than you presumed, other times
Heart-wrenching, like tears that don't want
To come out; your chest is more than pining
For ease. Sometimes change is forced upon
You like a cleanup in the wake
Of a disaster. But you go on
Heart open like your womb, waiting
For a change, a pulse, a sign of life.

Our Future Dear

You drive me to the ocean and I say leave
This current, with its salty bite, off shore.
On a rusted boat, we lack control of the oars
And weave a wake in waters tousled, upheave

The battleship of weight between a wife
And husband under pressures only found
In deep sea dives, far from an anchorage ground,
Our private submarine, our secret strife.

We sit on a dock to watch the line of light
And dark waters. I say that's where the sharks
Hide out. Like the lunar line, perhaps our mark,
The skill of being in constant flux, us shipwrights.

Back home the drugs are being shipped as we gear
Up for another round of IVF.
This time our hazy hope is our life vest,
Praying swim, stick, and stay, our future dear.

To Rest in the Potato Field

The worn, paint-chipped doors open to the corn
Fields stretch for acres, and under the clouds the kids
Play Marco Polo, veiled by stalks. We mourn
To Ashoken Waltz strummed by my dad. We bid
Farewell to Uncle Don, breathing the same
Uncropped potato dust that he once did.
We stroll through graves to find the family name.
I take pics of Esther's Covered Bridge and the church
In red — a valley staple, a constant flame.
A year of ruthless news stole time, it lurched
Us all and snatched the captain from the lake,
Cancer forcing him to catch his last yellow perch
Too soon. My pop-pop carries the urn to take
His older brother on one last walk, to rest
His ashes in the field and leave the ache
Behind. Though we're not born with safety vests,
We float with comfort, on seas of family ties.
The raindrops cry upon us. His ashes, blessed,
Are cast into the field, unreeled, a last sail.
And Grace flows out; he flies. Together we rise.

Bone Soup

"I'm sorry, I wasn't expecting you!" She laughs
With nervousness and tears. "I would have put
My wig on!" But her pale and shiny scalp
Brings no dis-ease to me, but rather faith
That she's got this battle underway. I hug
Her; she falls apart in my arms. Her tears, her bones,
But my weight the heaviest, not a girl anymore,
But a woman holding her grandma as a voice
Holds prayers in the back of a throat, a constant hum.

She drew me baths from sweet pea-scented pearls,
Played Pickup Sticks on the floor of the cabin, taught
Me how to slow time to a stop and take in all
One moment has to give. She gave me bowls
Of frozen berries and watched me climb the same
Oak tree my father did, played hide-and-seek
Among her hedge and garden on summer nights.
She caught me like a firefly and tucked
Me into sheets that never felt so safe.

Her friend is boiling broth for days. "Bone soup,"
She says, she'll drink between her treatments, a broth
So nutrient full it heals, and all I can pray
Is that bone soup will be her strawberries
In summertime, her steady hand in the tug
Of a game, her comfort hug from linen sheets,

Her spotter as she climbs this craggy tree.
If I could, I'd stop the ticking clock and be
Her broth, her elixir binding health to life.

A Whale in LOVE Park

When yesterday I stood inside LOVE Park,
I wished that you would feel the same as me.
Beneath the fountain's misty roar, we'd embark
To splash each other's clothes until we're free
And indulge in all this city's charm entails.
Instead our love is like the underground,
The grime that pulls in all directions, wails
And moans a lonely 52 Hertz sound.
It's not until the morning when we wake,
Settle in Jean's Café on Walnut Street,
And all I hear is the flip of griddle cakes
And the scrape of salty home fries over heat,
That I realize I'm in love *with* love, in love
With all I've found LOVE Fountain barren of.

The Orbit of Her

"If you want her, she's yours. It's ready for sale. Take a look inside. You can check out the foundation, make sure it's not falling in on itself. What do you plan to do with it?"

Before answering, he inhales deeply, city smog and smoke. "Create space, mainly. There's not enough of that around, ya know? But really, it's an investment that in the long run, hopefully, will pay off."

"Yeah, I hear you."

He writes a check for the space and hands it to the agent. He notices the building is kind of sad on the outside, slouching between a clock store and a jewelry store advertising diamonds for the month of April. "She's kind of rainy looking, but I'll take her," as she droops like the curve of an umbrella. But she's his now, and he's already planning what he'll do to improve the space.

First the man walks downtown. He's already downtown, but he walks further downtown, where the buildings are taller and full of pride. He sees a store called The Planetarium, and he purchases seeds of all the planets, as well as a couple more that might do well in the environment, the stubborn sadness that his building can't seem to forget. "We'll change that," he thinks to himself as the cashier wraps the seeds in a damp paper cloth and places them in a baggy to go.

"Keep 'em moist until you're ready to give life to them. Otherwise, Saturn might not get its rings, the moon its craters, and so on."

"Will do. They're going into the space today, so it won't be a problem."

Outside, it isn't much more cheerful than his old building. The raindrops are falling in a loss for the sky. He lights another joint and walks *up*town, as we'll call it, skipping the cracks on the sidewalk, feeling a little like a child who holds the entire universe in the palm of his hands. 314 Norfolk Ave. He reaches the door and steps into his space, but he jumps quickly back out onto the cement stoop, because something's just not right. He moves his hand across the door threshold, blackness; he pulls it out again. This time he stretches his leg into the building. Again — blackness. Even in the darkness, he can feel the sadness of her. Though he had invested in this space, he knows he's just a spectator. He wants to take the planets from his pocket, remembering the words from the clerk, but he doesn't have any pockets to find them in. Though, in the space in front of him, he sees a ball of fiery red, a blue and green marble catching glints of swirling light. In fact, he sees them all, the planets taking form and growing momentum before his eyes, or what would be his eyes, if he had them to identify with.

He becomes very sleepy and lies down. He can't even feel the floor, there's no sensation of falling, but he finds himself quite comfortable there. Thoughts begin to creep into his mind, the way fog travels down a riverbed in early morning. The thoughts are more vivid and tangible than the void his body is in, so they became very real. He thinks of the myriads of beings, the cycling, the meeting and the falling away. He sweats out what he doesn't need, like a shedding and then a rebirthing. He thinks of his mother, her eyes that held no secrets, her voice so very familiar, he had always sworn she'd been with him for lifetimes. His father weaves into his mind as well, the comfort he gave, equal to the feeling of the ground itself. He pictures a girl who encompasses these familiar qualities. In the blackness of the space and the vastness of his mind, he's drawn to her.

"I did, or I thought I did," he hears a girl's voice pulling him from his slumber-like high. He can't see her, but he sees Arcturus flickering in the blackness like a rainbow-colored sparkler. Not extinguishing the glow at all, but covering it softly, the Milky Way twirls and slowly takes a shape that he feels he should recognize. Mercury oozes hot iron, filling the shape before his eyes with blood and life force. The moon infiltrates this shape and transforms to emotions. The sun finds its space as the solar plexus, pulsating with confidence and warmth. And he begins to see her — a girl. But not just any girl. His love.

Her hair looks darker than usual, drenched in moist stars. His own skin is now glistening and dripping, as the falling stars become larger and more numerous. Below him he feels ground, solid and solacing. The stars, falling, turn to liquid, water now, gushing all around his feet and flowing in her direction. "I *thought* I needed space," she says. Her eyes have glints of color, the same as Neptune, a blue that could only exist in a celestial place. "But I didn't. I needed you to see me, really see me. For so long now, it has felt like you were just looking through me, but not at me. It felt like I had disappeared to you."

He doesn't say it now, though he knows. She *had* disappeared to him.

Like Blossoms

We sip cold beers from brown-tinted glass beside
The canal that runs perpendicular to brick
Row homes and narrow alleyways. Birds glide
Through the summer heat, and after a while we click,

Like the stonework in this town built years ago.
Our foundation, strong, uncovered, and weeded out,
Can now sustain our future plans, aglow
With a sweet, rekindled love. We talk about

The child we may or may not have, when in
A few more months the radiation will
Have fully left my body, my womb within,
Then safe to harbor life. That moment of thrill

Now in our field of view. We talk of health
Instead of sickness, a change so new to us.
It's almost frightening to have the talks we shelved,
The talks that came to be painful to discuss.

We reflect upon the marathon we've run
And turn our minds to future runs we'll take,
Through orchards blooming, trails
Under oak trees and sun,
Up mountains and along a crystal lake.

Our hands are together more than they're apart.

Our love, in balance, is both old and tenderly new.
I see him differently, more from the heart.
Both his and mine, like blossoms, a fuchsia hue.

Perennials

I wish that I were in
A different place in my life,
But here is where I am:
I'm in a waiting room,
Still awkward and left over
From being an uneasy child,
Not wanting to be seen.
I'll be sick in this waiting room,
A room full of women waiting
To be mothers. A goose and a gosling
Float in a painting on the wall.
They move swiftly through
A blooming floral reflection.
The gosling follows closely
Behind the mother's wing.
I'm already a mother, not
A good one, but they call
Me mom and sometimes mama,
Which is what I had imagined
When I was young. Right now,
My breasts are heavy from
A child I'll never have.
And nothing feels safe after
You lose a baby,
Especially your babies
Already planted and blossoming
Like summer salvia. You hold

Them closer even though
You think of them as perennials.
But our constants may only be
As lasting as a season.

A Summer's Night

My blue-eyed babies leave for summer break;
They take my smile pressed upon their faces.
They won't return until there's leaves to rake.
The Seven Sisters have guided me, tonight
The Big Dipper casts and scoops me up.
In a bowl of fish I swim and splash
Under a night sky shining deeply.
The surf echoes down the shore
Through what seems like a breezeway,
A long, narrow hallway between the bay
And the sea on either side. The sun dazzles
The waves and I inhale salt and wind.
I think she would have struck me dead
Had she answered me right then,
Asking about the chance of a future child.
I don't recall her words, only the colors
Pouring down on me, purple hues and
Imperfect pearls, and the children rushing in water
Part mermaid, part ocean, part pulse.

Porcelain

My daughter looks in the mirror and cries,
And I think, "God, not her too."
My heart shatters thinking what
She will endure over the years.
It's like turning the pages of a book
You're forced to read.
I want to color her in high self-esteem,
Smooth her mottled image into a clear reflection.
I'd give her my view of her if I could,
My pristine daughter, whose tender heart
Could heal the whole world if only —
If only believing in oneself was a noun,
And I could give it to her. Then maybe.

The Thick of It

She tried to gouge her emotions out
Through the veins in her arms.
There's not enough mental health
Facilities in our country,
But I have to believe she'll be one who is saved.
I bring her, a slouching pile of bones,
To the treatment facility. Her eyes look even larger
Now that she's lost more weight.
They're haunting and half empty,
And it'll keep me up at night
As I try to navigate healing,
Rein back in the chaos
Her disorders have spun us into.
I'll think about how all the nurses know her,
And that the third time was not a charm.
I want normalcy, but I know I won't have it.
The karma plays out and I get worn out to the point
Where all I see when I look in the mirror is a tattered,
Empty shell. But I'm her mother.
And if anyone can help save her, it's me.
So I swallow my own pills for depression,
Anxiety, and bipolar,
And I wake up another day,
Pray I'm another day stronger, wiser, and caring.
Motherhood, this thing I've been doing
For sixteen years and still have no idea.
It can bring a kind of backwards walk,

The way you must venture along the road
Into your past to find the way to your future.
I'm walking back, I'm searching forward,
Trying to find answers for her future from my past.

Flow of Rhythm

The first night I dreamt of wind and rain and you.
Dividing in a Petri dish, a dance
So secretive as you grew into tissue,
And I prepared to take this game of chance.

The rain turned to months of sleet and snow.
You stuck. I called you our frosty,
Thawed. A flickering beat,
Then flutters and shifts.
You made your mark, you were tucked
In me; I changed to fit you before we meet.

You came in, a gentle warrior, bringing calm
You never want to leave my arms, a gift.
To all our wounds you are the prayed-for balm.
Time spent with you, floating in a dream, adrift

In these early days where everything's anew.
Yes, still, I'm giddy with the sweet thought of you.

Eclipse

The moon cast a blue shadow
The day you turned a week.
You woke and cried and shifted in my hold,
Not used to the space, the lack of walls.
Years into this life, there are days
The space still startles me.
The tears swell for no reason and I shift
Your weight from one side of my chest to the other.
I retreat to my blue-walled bedroom
Where we'll stay for weeks
While I wait for you to mature.
I walked away just as the blue shade peaked
And just before the shadows dimpled and crescented.
Instead, I study the dimples in your hands
Tuck your fragile body into my curved hold,
And let tears of missing out fall onto the swaddle.

The Beginning of the Pandemic

On the last day, they sit on a blanket
In the backyard, dog intently sitting by.
The air is fairly still until it stirs when new life arrives.
I want to cry, all day, but it won't come out,
Like rain clouds in passing.
I watch the field turn green,
I pick perennials from the front yard.
I run the sink until the water is cool,
And I wash the garden from my hands.
I read an article on India, and tears well up, again.
On repeat, I can't hold back.
They make s'mores with the last bar of chocolate.
He smiles ear to ear.
The fire glows orange against their new love.
Crackling fills the air, sweet sugar heated black.
It's a grief I've never felt,
Not knowing what's to come.

Twenty-Twenty

Finding calm in the storm.
Making sure loved ones are okay.
Making sure I'm okay
So I can take care of loved ones.
Restless. Board games. Cooking meals
We've never cooked before.
All sitting at one table. Calm.
Birds feeding and chirping.
Nap. Skipping a nap.
Going on a run and noticing
New sprouts, new blooms.
Rest. Stare off. Fight anxiety.
Calm anxiety with conversation.
Conversations being held
That never would have happened.
Family. Peace. A love like I've never felt.
News. Lots of news. Fighting it with care.
Looking forward. Knowing this is temporary.
Getting to know my kids in new ways.
Isolation. But isolation with the ones I love.
Learning. Learning to be strong and calm
And find the center of the storm so all can benefit.
Ripples. We're all so more connected
Than I could ever previously conceive.
Love, cook for one another.
Wash hands on repeat.
Try not to worry about

Everything being sold out.
Inhale and exhale, we are all one.
Fold laundry, lay down,
Close my eyes that hurt.
Rest. Repeat. Pick my little one up
And give kisses and tickles.
Play, laugh, love fully. Offer comfort.
Watch my loved ones grow. Grow with them.
Become in sync with growth, with love.
Think about others, often.
Pray, deep, deeper than the well outside.
Deeper than I'm used to.
Pray like we are all one, because we are.

In Isolation

It's day whatever.
Caiden's running with muddy boots
The length of the yard.
The sun is setting on another stressful day.
He wants to jump and sing and play.
I wipe the wrinkles from my forehead
And hold him close in the early spring air.
We are all experiencing a collective karma.
I think my therapist needed to talk
More than me today.
We talked about death, prayer, meditation, and Phowa.
I sent her prayers that I play on repeat.
I'm thankful for the land around us,
The breeze through the mulberry tree,
The breath in my lungs.
Today the wind is like to ocean,
And I brace myself for it.
The wind is more like a breath, it ebbs and flows.
I weave with it. We make a web,
A pact to keep going.
We are growing, growing into one.
We always were one. We are falling back in sync.
I'm scared, but together we are sound, safe.

Ready Room

I wake up late.
He held my hand
All night. I awake
Within those same
Blue walls that tuck
Me away each night.
I awake to the word
'Swim' after a dream
That my golden fish, now white
From illness and age,
Is no different from
My own child.
My aunt and I
Drive to the temple
To renounce our day
To a selfless activity.
And things I thought
Had mattered float
Away as beads
Of sweat drip down
My face, and a peace
Rushes in. A cool
Blue water, the tint
Of my walls, washes
Me clean. And maybe
It's just what I need,
To be neck deep

In contemplation
With heart and mind
Braided, humbled
By my aunt's presence.
And when she says
"It's a good day for laps,"
I contemplate
How she keeps on swimming,
And more often than not,
I think of stopping.
But today there's sun
And water and air
And all I need
For growth. My heart
Is full, my head
Is emptied. And swimming
Doesn't seem so daunting
Of a task. This wave,
This current has me.
I smile and say, "Yes."
It's a good day for laps.